The Autobiography of
Rear Admiral John A. Dahlgren

EDITED BY PETER C. LUEBKE

Published by
Naval History and Heritage Command
805 Kidder Breese Street SE
Washington Navy Yard, DC 20374-5060

Book Design by Eleni Giannakopoulos

U.S. GOVERNMENT OFFICIAL EDITION NOTICE

AUTHENTICATED U.S. GOVERNMENT INFORMATION GPO

Use of ISBN

This is an official U.S. Government edition of this publication and is herein identified to certify its authenticity. This title's print edition is cataloged under ISBN 978-1-943604-18-0. A Section 508–compliant PDF is cataloged under ISBN 978-1-943604-19-7. The title's e-book edition is catalogued under ISBN 978-1-943604-48-7.

Library of Congress Cataloging-in Publication Data

Dahlgren, John A.
The Autobiography of Rear Admiral John A. Dahlgren: Edited by Peter C. Luebke Dahlgren. – U.S. Government official edition.
Pages cm. – (The U.S. Navy and the Civil War)
Includes bibliographical references and index.
ISBN 978-1-943604-18-0 (Softcover alk.paper) — ISBN 978-1-943604-19-7 (508-compliant pdf) — ISBN 978-1-943604-48-7 (E-book)

For Sale by Superintendent of Documents, U.S. Government Publishing Office
Internet: Bookstore.gpo.gov; Phone: toll free 1-866-512-1800; DC area 202-512-1800;
Fax: 201-512-2104
Mail: Stop SSOP, Washington, DC 20402-001

CONTRIBUTIONS TO NAVAL HISTORY NO. 8

The Autobiography of

REAR ADMIRAL JOHN A. DAHLGREN

EDITED BY PETER C. LUEBKE

Naval History and Heritage Command
Department of the Navy
Washington, DC
2018

CONTENTS

FOREWORD

In the first years of the Civil War, President Abraham Lincoln would occasionally get on his horse, ride over to the Washington Navy Yard and pass time with then–Captain John Dahlgren. Dahlgren would test-fire his latest developments in naval ordnance down the Anacostia River, which fascinated Lincoln. This pastime required some degree of courage on Lincoln's part, given the disaster that occurred on the Potomac River aboard USS *Princeton* in 1844, when a new "long gun" exploded during a demonstration firing killing the Secretary of the Navy, Secretary of State, and several others, while President John Tyler was aboard. In this case, however, Lincoln had reason for confidence that Dahlgren knew what he was doing because he had been at the forefront of naval ordnance advances for more than a decade. Lincoln and Dahlgren shared an unlikely friendship, given their very different personalities. Dahlgren was not above using their friendship to his advantage. Lincoln upset standard protocol, intervening directly to get Dahlgren promoted to rear admiral and what Dahlgren coveted the most—a major sea-going command with the South Atlantic Blockading Squadron.

The period between the end of the Mexican War and the start of the Civil War was a low point for the U.S. Navy in terms of budgets, with few operational ships, many of which were undermanned with challenges finding enough qualified Sailors. It was, however, an era of profound technological changes in warfare at sea, which would be greatly accelerated by the Civil War. Chief among these was the beginning of a shift from sail to steam, the creation of armored warships (ironclads), and the invention of exploding shells for cannon. Although the Navy struggled to afford to put the new technologies to sea, Dahlgren in particular led the way in developing much of the technology, particularly in the realm of cannons, ammunition, and other naval ordnance.

Dahlgren began his naval career as a scientist. He concentrated on technological advances in Europe and how they might be brought to the U.S. Navy. This study led to the creation of a new boat howitzer for Navy use, new ideas about ship armament and design, and the invention of the ingenious Dahlgren gun, which became the Navy's chief ordnance during the Civil War.

Dahlgren's scientific activities began with his work on the U.S. Coast Survey and its effort to map the coastline of the country. Because of this and his study of ordnance, he was invited to join scientific societies, beginning his cultivation of a much wider range of business, press, academic, and political leaders. The resulting influence did not, however, lead initially to command at sea.

At the outbreak of the Civil War, as commandant of the Washington Navy

Yard, Dahlgren quickly moved on his own initiative to improve the defenses of the river approaches to the capital city. He acted energetically to organize defensive details to protect the yard and its military stores from Confederate threat, at a time when many did not completely grasp the threat, because of the pervasive over-confidence that the war would be short.

Not surprisingly, most of Dahlgren's autobiography concentrates on the Civil War period. He writes extensively about his own exploits and those of his sons. One of his sons, Ulric, served in the Union Army with distinction and was killed during a controversial cavalry raid on Richmond in 1864. Another of his sons, Charles, served with the Navy on the Mississippi River in operations against Vicksburg, where he gained experience putting his father's inventions to practical use. In his autobiography, Dahlgren also takes time to recognize the heroism of Union officers and men during the war. For example, he mentions the valor of Commander James Ward, the first Union naval officer killed in the war, in action against Confederate batteries, as well as the bravery of Sailors during battles in and around Charleston Harbor.

As commander of the South Atlantic Blockading Squadron, Dahlgren's inability to bring about the fall of Charleston from the sea led a number of contemporary critics to suggest that his abilities as a technical officer significantly exceeded his abilities as a combat commander. Some of this was due to jealousy as to how he came to be in command of the squadron, but some was justified. Dahlgren also faced numerous obstacles, as the Confederates energetically adopted technologies such as mines, torpedo boats, and a submarine. Friction with U.S. Army commanders, which was not unique to Dahlgren, didn't help either. Despite these challenges, the South Atlantic Blockading Squadron gradually cut the Confederacy off from foreign supplies. Charleston fell in 1865 with the approach of General William T. Sherman's force, but Dahlgren and the Navy had contributed greatly to this victory.

Dahlgren's legacy in the Navy was profound and lasting, primarily for his role in designing and developing the weapons and ammunition that enabled the Union Navy to emerge victorious at sea and on the inland waterways during the Civil War. Because of this, when the Naval Surface Warfare Center Dahlgren was established during World War I in 1918, and which to this day designs and tests most of the Navy's shipboard weapons, it was named in honor of John A. Dahlgren.

RADM Samuel J. Cox, USN (Retired)
Director of Naval History
Curator of the Navy
Director, Naval History and Heritage Command

INTRODUCTION

Among the naval heroes of the Civil War, Rear Admiral John Adolphus Bernard Dahlgren remains largely unknown. Part of this rests upon his sometimes difficult personality and self-promotion that aggravated his fellow officers; the other part of this lies upon his failure to take the Confederate city of Charleston by naval force. Dahlgren's solid service during the siege of Charleston and in command of the South Atlantic Blockading Squadron did much to assure Union victory during the war, but it contained no stirring episodes that became legendary, such as those of David Glasgow Farragut at the Battle of Mobile Bay. Yet Dahlgren, and his autobiography, remains important today.

This book presents a transcription of an autobiography that Dahlgren wrote shortly after the Civil War. In it, he gives an account of his entire career. He describes the multiple innovations he introduced into the U.S. Navy. His career coincided with the important transition from sail to steam propulsion and the change from solid shot to cannon that fired explosive shells. Dahlgren's service demonstrates that naval officers have always confronted technological challenges and have attempted to overcome them, often against significant bureaucratic barriers from both within and without the Navy. During the Civil War, he also faced the shift in naval warfare from wooden-hulled ships to ironclad vessels. He assumed command at Charleston in 1863 after the ironclad squadron under Rear Admiral Samuel Francis Du Pont failed to live up to the impossible expectation that ironclads alone could capture the city. Indeed, Dahlgren grappled with how best to use the new technology in operations with the Army against an unparalleled concentration of Confederate fortifications. Beyond learning how to employ the new vessels, he confronted new kinds of asymmetric warfare used by the Confederate defenders. Dahlgren and the Navy dealt with underwater mines, known at the time as torpedoes, the first successful military submarine, and semi-submerged torpedo boats. Finally, he wrote frequently of his often-bitter relations with Major General Quincy A. Gillmore, who commanded the Union Army during much of the Charleston campaign. The difficulty of achieving cooperation between two forces without a unified command authority provided a negative example for joint operations.

In addition to his own experiences, Dahlgren wrote of the heroism, courage, and dedication of those under his command or those he knew. He discusses the early operations of Commodore James Ward, who lost his life in 1861 engaged against Confederate shore batteries. He also describes the heroism of his officers and men during the operations around Charleston, from those on his staff to the extraordinary actions of his Sailors.

Before the Civil War, Dahlgren stood out as one of the foremost innovators in the Navy. Born in Philadelphia on 13 November 1809, he began his career in the Navy as midshipman in 1826. After a cruise aboard *Macedonian*, he embarked upon a long period of fruitful devotion to science. He advocated for the use of steam power, served on the United States Coast Survey, designed new kinds of ordnance, and subsequently gained prominence within the Navy.[1]

The outbreak of the Civil War found Dahlgren in the Bureau of Ordnance at the Washington Navy Yard. With the resignation of Navy officers who went South, he soon found himself in charge of the Navy Yard and energetically embarked in securing it against secessionists. By virtue of his long service in Washington, DC, Dahlgren also cultivated relationships with politicians. Over the first few years of the war, he became close friends with President Abraham Lincoln. Because of this, Dahlgren was promoted to the head of the Ordnance Bureau, received promotion to rear admiral, and obtained a major sea command during the war.[2]

His rise sparked animosity with his fellow officers and politicians. They viewed him as a self-promoter who had capitalized upon his friendship with Lincoln. Gideon Welles, the Secretary of the Navy, confided in his diary of Dahlgren, that "He desires, beyond almost any one, the high honors of his profession, and has his appetite stimulated by the partiality of the President."[3] Dahlgren had spent most of his career on shore, and thus ran afoul of those who had devoted their careers to long, hard service at sea. Welles wrote in 1863, when considering Dahlgren for command at Charleston, "older officers who have had vastly greater sea-service would feel aggrieved at his selection and find ready sympathizers among the juniors."[4] These complaints centered on Dahlgren's personality, rather than his courage. A senator from Iowa averred, "I have no affection for the man and not much respect. He is a courtier; he is doubtless brave; but he is, in my conviction, the most conceited man in the Navy."[5] Despite the complaints

[1] Robert J. Schneller Jr., *A Quest for Glory: A Biography of Rear Admiral John A. Dahlgren* (Annapolis, MD: Naval Institute Press, 1996), 1–175.

[2] Ibid., 176–247.

[3] William E. Gienapp and Erica L. Gienapp, eds., *The Civil War Diary of Gideon Welles, Lincoln's Secretary of the Navy: The Original Manuscript Edition* (Urbana: The Knox College Lincoln Studies Center and the University of Illinois Press, 2014), 140.

[4] Ibid., 196–97.

[5] James Grimes Wilson to Samuel Francis Du Pont, 1 July 1863, in Samuel Francis Du Pont, *Samuel Francis Du Pont: A Selection from His Civil War Letters: Vol. 3, The Repulse: 1863-1865*,

from fellow officers and the skepticism of Welles, after much pleading, Dahlgren received command of the South Atlantic Blockading Squadron in 1863.

On 6 July 1863, Dahlgren took command of the South Atlantic Blockading Squadron, relieving Rear Admiral Samuel Francis Du Pont. Du Pont had led a failed attack on Charleston on 7 April 1863; it had been "supposed to showcase the strength of the monitors" and both "Welles and Lincoln were under political pressure for a victory. Feeling that the public needed to be satisfied, these two men pushed" for the attack.[6] As a result, Du Pont was ousted and Dahlgren replaced him.

With this appointment, Dahlgren received what he had always wanted, a sea command where he could gain greater glory for himself and the Navy. Charleston and the South Atlantic Blockading Squadron, though, proved a poor vehicle for realizing this ambition. As with Du Pont before him, Dahlgren was thwarted by the strong Confederate defenses, poor coordination with the Union Army, and conflicting imperatives from Washington. During the early months of his command, he enjoyed some success; his monitors damaged Fort Sumter and the Union took control of Morris Island on 7 September. After that, however, progress faltered because of the still-robust Confederate defenses. Dahlgren and his squadron turned their attention to the coastal blockade.[7]

With the failure to take Charleston, acrimony erupted between Dahlgren and the Union Army commander, Major General Quincy Gillmore. Accounts began appearing in newspapers that questioned Dahlgren's leadership, which Dahlgren suspected originated from Gillmore's headquarters. While Gillmore denied that he had the sympathetic articles published, they had indeed emanated from those around him. This affair poisoned relations between the two leaders and doomed Army-Navy cooperation at Charleston. The city fell only when Major General William T. Sherman's march through the Carolinas rendered it indefensible from the land.[8]

After the war, Dahlgren wrote multiple accounts in an attempt to set the record straight. He most likely wrote this autobiography in 1866 at the behest of

---

ed. John D. Hayes (Ithaca, NY: Published for the Eleutherian Mills Historical Library by Cornell University Press, 1969), 191.

6 Robert M. Browning Jr., *Success Is All that Was Expected: The South Atlantic Blockading Squadron during the Civil War* (Washington, DC: Brassey's, 2002), 210.

7 Ibid., 215–359; Schneller, A Quest for Glory, 251–320.

8 Schneller, *A Quest for Glory*, 269–73.

Joel T. Headley.[9] Headley, who had written earlier histories of George Washington, Napoleon Bonaparte, Ulysses S. Grant, and William T. Sherman, turned his attention to Union naval leaders. He desired to "bring out into distinct relief the important actions of our navy" as well as "to give a personal history of the brave officers who covered themselves and the nation with honor." In preparing the book, Headley noted that "in almost every case, the facts and personal details in the biographical sketches have been furnished either by the commanders themselves, or their friends, with their approval."[10] His chapter on Dahlgren quotes from this autobiographical manuscript and at times lifts entire sentences without attribution. In addition, several other idiosyncrasies establish that Headley based his sketch of Dahlgren on this manuscript. Most prominently, Headley renders the name of the monitor *Catskill* as "*Katskill*," just as Dahlgren did.

Exactly how or when Dahlgren met Headley remains unknown, but the two travelled in the same social circles. Dahlgren knew New York publishers such as David Van Nostrand.[11] In addition, his activities in various scientific associations put him in contact with other scientists, historians, and writers. Either through one of these associates, or directly, Headley solicited biographical details from Dahlgren. The manuscript here represented Dahlgren's response. It also stands as the longest sustained personal description of his life by himself, and as such is important in establishing what he thought was important about his career.

In crafting his autobiographical sketch, Dahlgren relied not only on his own recollections, but also on contemporary primary source materials. Like modern historians, he used supporting sources to buttress his points. He enjoyed authority to comment on the events because he had been an eyewitness, but he also cited extensively from others' accounts and contemporary records to corroborate his points.[12] This corroboration remained central, because Dahlgren sought to counter Gillmore's allegations that the Navy had been responsible for the Union

[9] In the Dahlgren manuscript, there is a pencil notation that reads "Oct 12 1866." This might indicate when Dahlgren finished the manuscript or when Headley received it.

[10] J[oel] T[aylor] Headley, *Farragut and Our Naval Commanders* (New York: E. B. Treat & Co., 1867), vii, ix.

[11] Van Nostrand published some of Dahlgren's other writings. When Dahlgren and Andrew H. Foote met to discuss the replacement of Samuel Francis Du Pont at Charleston, they met at Van Nostrand's house. Spencer C. Tucker, *Andrew Foote: Civil War Admiral on Western Waters* (Annapolis, MD: Naval Institute Press, 2000), 202.

[12] For more on eyewitness authority and the practice of history in the 19th century, see: Ann Fabian, *The Unvarnished Truth: Personal Narratives in Nineteenth-Century America* (Berkeley: University of California Press, 2000); and Eileen Ka-May Cheng, *The Plain and Noble Garb of Truth: Nationalism and Impartiality in American Historical Writing, 1784–1860* (Athens: University of Georgia Press, 2008).

failure to take Charleston. Dahlgren sought to move the debate from one of conflicting personalities to one where careful consideration of evidence would reveal Gillmore was lying.

In addition to his refutation of Gillmore, Dahlgren focuses on several other themes. He notes his friendship with Lincoln and movingly discusses their relationship. He also carefully notes the heroic performance of subordinates and other naval officers. Although at times his manuscript demonstrates the conceit that others identified in him, it also shows that he sought to give others their due. Besides commenting on the actions of naval officers, Dahlgren wrote with pride of the accomplishments of his son Ulric who served first as a volunteer aide and then received an officer's commission in the Army and became an accomplished cavalryman. He died in early 1864 while leading a raid on Richmond, one that became controversial as orders were discovered on Ulric's body that called for the assassination of Confederate President Jefferson Davis. Dahlgren describes these events in his autobiography and displays obvious pride that his children also served the Union during the war.

This autobiography represents but one piece of Dahlgren's postwar efforts to burnish his reputation and dispel falsehoods. He wrote at length to other authors, often drawing upon the same materials he used in his autobiography. Although he died before he completed them, he worked on a memoir of his son Ulric's life as well as his own autobiography.[13]

Dahlgren corresponded extensively with historian John William Draper. Draper, who had written one volume of a multi-volume history of the Civil War, asked Dahlgren for an account of the siege of Charleston. Dahlgren responded with enthusiasm. Draper promised to "give this paper, as also any other you may send, all my attention writing that part of my volume to which they refer."[14] Dahlgren subsequently kept up a steady stream of material to Draper and also pointed him to published accounts. In these efforts, as in this autobiography, he sought to present his own point of view with as much impartiality as possible. As he told Draper, "It is very gratifying to know that what I have written has been

---

[13] [John A.] Dahlgren, *Memoir of Ulric Dahlgren* (Philadelphia: J. B. Lippincott, 1872) and Madeleine Vinton Dahlgren, *Memoir of John A. Dahlgren, Rear Admiral United States Navy* (Boston: James R. Osgood, 1882).

[14] Quotation from John William Draper to John A. Dahlgren, 7 October 1868, John A. Dahlgren Papers, Library of Congress. See also: John William Draper to John A. Dahlgren, 14 September 1868, John A. Dahlgren Papers, Library of Congress; John A. Dahlgren to John William Draper, 17 September 1868, Draper Family Papers, Library of Congress; and John William Draper to John A. Dahlgren, 22 September 1868, John A. Dahlgren Papers, Library of Congress.

so well considered in its Historic aspect—It has been my endeavor to follow fact, and I hope to a proper conclusion—I feel sure that time will confirm all I have written."[15] Ultimately, Dahlgren sent Draper an account of Charleston of several hundred pages, as well as shorter documents. Undoubtedly overwhelmed by this effusion, Draper pledged to include what he could but observed that "the limited space obliges me to condense very much, but I still hope to be able to present those facts sufficiently."[16]

When Draper's book appeared, Dahlgren was pleased with the results. He thanked the author for "the space you have allowed to the operations that concern myself . . . which will dispel much of the unjust impressions that have persisted in regard to the Naval operations off Charleston." He wrote that "I congratulate you on the completion of this great work in the true spirit of the 'Philosophy of History,'" which was a reference to the historical method based on the comparison of source materials to establish the truth that Draper had used in his previous books.[17]

In another instance, Dahlgren engaged in an exchange with William W. H. Davis, who wrote an early history of the 104th Pennsylvania Infantry Regiment, a unit that had served at Charleston.[18] Upon reading the book, Dahlgren wrote a letter to Davis, fulminating that "some statements . . . appear . . . which are highly unjust and derogatory to myself, and to the Naval force which I commanded in 1863 and subsequently." These statements dealt with the issue of the supposed agreement between Gillmore and the Navy Department that if the Army could suppress Fort Sumter, the ironclads would enter the harbor and take Charleston. Dahlgren refuted the idea that he had received any such instructions, and buttressed his point with communications to the Navy Department, the *Report on Armored Vessels*, contemporary histories of the Civil War, and a letter he had received from Major General William T. Sherman. At the end of his lengthy letter, Dahlgren concluded "to remark on the injustice done generally to the Navy by the brief and imperfect mention which its hard service receives,

[15] John A. Dahlgren to John William Draper, 14 December 1868, in Draper Family Papers, Library of Congress.

[16] John William Draper to John A. Dahlgren, 27 October 1868, John A. Dahlgren Papers, Library of Congress.

[17] John A. Dahlgren to John William Draper, 14 March 1870, Draper Family Papers, Library of Congress.

[18] W. W. H. Davis, *History of the 104th Pennsylvania Regiment, from August 22nd, 1861, to September 20th, 1864* (Philadelphia: James B. Rodgers, 1866).

with small exception, in the various narrations of the events of the rebellion."[19] In this exchange, Dahlgren sought to demonstrate that he, and the men under his command, had done as well they could have.

Although Dahlgren pressed his case with Davis, the former colonel remained unconvinced by the admiral's arguments. Davis countered Dahlgren's sources with one his own, claiming that "one in high authority, who heard what was said" informed him of the agreement between Gillmore and the Navy Department. Against Dahlgren's allegations that Davis simply parroted Gillmore's book, Davis stated, "I have never seen nor read [it]." Davis closed by pointing out that he had not commented on Dahlgren personally, only on the actions of the Navy Department. He thought "that General Gillmore and yourself were ordered on a most important enterprise without instruction" and "this proves the extremely loose manner in which the government conducted the war."[20] The correspondence with Davis indicates the struggle that Dahlgren faced in protecting his reputation. As one of Dahlgren's biographers has noted, "Dahlgren would refight the siege of Charleston on paper over and over again . . . these efforts resolved nothing and served no useful purpose."[21]

After the end of the war, Dahlgren continued his naval career. In 1866, he was placed in command of the South Pacific Squadron, where he remained until 1868. After that, he returned to Washington as chief of the Bureau of Ordnance. In 1869 he took command of the Washington Navy Yard, and held that position until he died of heart failure on 12 July 1870.[22]

The Text

This volume provides Dahlgren's autobiography. It has been annotated with explanatory footnotes that identify the sources Dahlgren used and direct the reader to further information. This book includes two additional documents as appendices. The first contains a letter from Sherman to Dahlgren written soon after the war. In it, Sherman offers a vindication of Dahlgren's performance at

[19] John A. Dahlgren to W. W. H. Davis, 8 October 1869, John Dahlgren Letterbooks, John A. Dahlgren Papers, Library of Congress.

[20] W. W. H. Davis to John A. Dahlgren, 10 December 1869, John A. Dahlgren Papers, Library of Congress. Gillmore's book included printed versions of his correspondence with Dahlgren; see Q. A. Gillmore, *Engineer and Artillery Operations Against the Defences of Charleston Harbor in 1863; Comprising the Descent Upon Morris Island, the Demolition of Fort Sumter, the Reduction of Forts Wagner and Gregg. With Observations on Heavy Ordnance, Fortifications, Etc.* (New York: D. Van Nostrand, 1865), 317–49.

[21] Schneller, *A Quest for Glory*, 324.

[22] Ibid., 321–64.

Charleston, apparently solicited by Dahlgren as a way to counter Gillmore's criticisms. Dahlgren references it in his autobiography several times and drew upon it in other postwar writings. The second appendix contains Dahlgren's description of the Confederate defenses at Charleston Harbor. Written for Draper, it presents a more thorough description of the Confederate fortifications than appears in the autobiography.

Editorial Method

So far as possible, this book provides an unaltered transcription of Dahlgren's 279-page autobiographical manuscript, now in the collections of the Navy Department Library at the Washington Navy Yard. Original punctuation and spelling have been retained. The following lists exceptions made. Ships' names have been italicized. Cancelled passages have been deleted silently, though in cases where the deleted content has particular significance, it is mentioned in a note. Dahlgren frequently used asterisks to make his own footnotes or cite his sources; they have been included in the notes section, prefaced by his initials, "JAD:" with the content in quotation marks to differentiate them from the editor's notes. Following the convention of the nineteenth century, when Dahlgren quoted long passages, he indicated so with quotation marks at the beginning of each line; these quotations have been rendered in modern style. Dahlgren's running heads at the top of each page, which give the year, have been removed. Finally, the handful of editorial insertions made in-text are indicated with brackets. The use of "sic" has been avoided.

Acknowledgments

A book such as this requires many people to pull together. Many have helped. At the Naval History and Heritage Command (NHHC), Dr. Gregory Bereiter checked my transcriptions and offered comments on annotation. Also at NHHC, Christopher B. Havern Sr. and Dr. Richard Hulver reviewed the annotations and gave their suggestions. Thomas Biggs helped with research of the illustrations. Both Tim Bostic and Davis Elliott of the Navy Department Library helped find crucial documents and books. Dr. Kristina Giannotta and Scott Anderson of the Histories Branch at NHHC provided much encouragement and support for this project. Charles E. Brodine Jr. reviewed the manuscript with his customary care. Jim Caiella and Brent Hunt of the Communication and Outreach Division took the manuscript to publication, improving it along the way.

The staffs of the Library of Congress and the National Archives at College Park provided assistance.

Dr. Robert M. Browning Jr. and Dr. Michael J. Crawford served as spectacular outside readers, offering critiques and commentary that saved me from many errors.

Short Title List

Sources referenced can be found in the bibliography. Abbreviations used for several sources are listed below. In the notes, the citation will use the abbreviation followed by the volume number.

JCCW *Report of the Joint Committee on the Conduct of the War*. 8 vols. Washington, DC: Government Printing Office, 1863–1866. Reprint, Wilmington, NC: Broadfoot Publishing, 2002. 9 vols.

OR *The War of the Rebellion: A Compilation of the Official Records of the Union and Confederate Armies*. 128 vols. Washington, DC: Government Printing Office, 1880–1901. All citations to Series 1 unless otherwise noted.

ORN *Official Records of the Union and Confederate Navies in the War of the Rebellion*. 31 vols. Washington, DC: Government Printing Office, 1894–1922. All citations to Series 1 unless otherwise noted.

CHAPTER 1

Early Years, 1809-1846

R. Admiral J. A. Dahlgren

Born—Novem. 1809[1] at Philadelphia on the spot now stands the City Exchange corner of Walnut & 3d

On the mothers side—the family had been among the early residents and possessed considerable property—the Grandfather (Rowan) had served in the War of Independence and was at the battles of Princeton and Germantown—[2]

Mr Bernard Dahlgren the father—was a native of Sweden—afterwards resident of Philad—and a merchant well known there for his ability and great integrity—had been educated at Upsala and was a ripe Scholar—Ancient and Modern languages—Sciences &c He died on the high road to wealth[3]—

The eldest son (John) succeeded in obtaining a Midshipman's warrant after a struggle which for a year seemed hopeless—

Date of Warrant Feb. 1st 1826—[4]

Served about Six years as a Midsn. first cruise was in the frigate *Macedonian*

---

[1] John Adolphus Bernard Dahlgren was born on 13 November 1809.

[2] John A. Dahlgren's mother was Martha Rowan, who had married Bernhard Dahlgren on 19 November 1808. Rowan's father, James Rowan, had served as a commissary during the American Revolution. Madeleine Vinton Dahlgren, *Memoir of John A. Dahlgren: Rear-Admiral United States Navy* (Boston: James R. Osgood and Company, 1882), 8–9

[3] Bernhard Ulrik Dahlgren was born on 12 May 1784. He left Sweden in 1804, after his agitation for republicanism ran afoul of the monarchy. He traveled to Spain and arrived in New York in December 1806. He made his living as a merchant and also served as the Swedish Consul in Philadelphia. He died in 1824. Ibid., 7–8.

[4] When his father died, John was only 14. He acted on a long-held desire to join the Navy, and beginning in 1824 supporters began sending letters recommending Dahlgren's appointment. Dahlgren himself wrote in February 1825 to Samuel L. Southard, Secretary of the Navy, stating that "having long been anxious to adopt as a profession the naval service of my country, and being sustained in my wishes by the kindness of many of my respectable friends, I beg leave to solicit the appointment of Midshipman in the Navy of the United States." Ibid., 11–16.

Swiss surveyor Ferdinand R. Hassler served as the first superintendent of the U.S. Coast Survey.

Library of Congress, Prints and Photographs Division, LC-DIG-pga-06411.

commanded by Com. Biddle—being the very ship captured from the British by Com. Decatur—Com. Biddle who now commanded had served in the war of 1812 and captured the Br. Brig *Penguin*—very severe disciplinarian—& peculiar but a brave and good officer[5]

1832

J.A.D. passed examination and received Warrant of Passed Midshipman dated April 28th 1832—his mathematical proficiency was the cause of his being ordered to the Coast survey then being re-established under Mr. Hassler—at that time perhaps the ablest Mathematician in the country—Mr. H. was as excentric as he was able.[6]

1834

J.A.D. passed on this duty 1834–1835–1836 and 1837-in the various work of

[5] On 25 March 1815, Capt. James Biddle, commanding *Hornet*, captured HM brig *Penguin* off the Tristan da Cunha Islands. For Commo. Stephen Decatur's capture of HMS *Macedonian* on 25 October 1812, see William S. Dudley, ed., *The Naval War of 1812: A Documentary History*, Vol. 1, (Washington, DC: Naval Historical Center, 1985), 548–53. See also David F. Long, *Sailor Diplomat: A Biography of Commodore James Biddle, 1783-1848* (Boston: Northeastern University Press, 1983); and James Tertius de Kay, *Chronicles of the Frigate* Macedonian: *1809-1922* (New York: W.W. Norton and Company, 1995).

[6] Swiss scientist Ferdinand Rudolf Hassler superintended the U.S. Coastal Survey. See also Hugh Richard Slotten, *Patronage, Practice, and the Culture of American Science: Alexander Dallas Bache and the U.S. Coast Survey* (New York: Cambridge University Press, 1994).

field and office—the most notable of which events were:—J.A.D. was selected to serve in the triangulation of the Survey—and to assist in the Astronomical operations as well as the measurement of the Base on Long Island under Mr. Hassler himself—This was the first base-line ever measured scientifically in America That of Mason & Dixon being a chain & compass measurement.

1835

—Mr. Hassler afterwards chose J.A.D. to make the counter calculations of the Base which were to compare with and verify his own—

1836

In May assisted to observe solar eclipse at Westhills, a station of the Survey—there engaged in secondary Triangulation till autumn—[7]

Navy Department offered J A D. the appointment of Sailing Master to the *Macedonian* the flagship of exploring expedition under Com. Jones to South Seas; declined, because dissensions had arisen between the Com. Officers and J A D. did not believe the Expedition would ever proceed as then organised—which conjecture proved correct—It was entirely re-organised and sailed under the command of Commodore Wilkes—[8]

In autumn was detailed from the secondary triangulation to assist in the first trials of the great Theodolite just completed by Troughton[9] for Mr. Hassler—it had a diam. of three feet and compound Microscopes instead of verniers for

[7] A theodolite measured vertical and horizontal planes, and provided more accurate measurements of angles than other instruments, which in turn allowed for more precise trigonomic calculations in geographic surveys. The Coast Survey set up a station at West Hills, Long Island, NY. F[erdinand] R[udolf] Hassler, *Principal Documents Relating to the Survey of the Coast of the United States, Since 1816* (New York: William van Norden, 1834), 112.

[8] The U.S. Exploring Expedition to the Pacific had been organized under Capt. Thomas ap Catesby Jones. It ran into organizational problems due to the poor condition of the ships assigned to expedition, as well as conflict between the naval officers and scientists. Ultimately, Jones resigned and the expedition proceeded under the command of Lt. Charles Wilkes. For more on the organization of the expedition, see Gene A. Smith, *Thomas ap Catesby Jones: Commodore of Manifest Destiny* (Annapolis, MD. Naval Institute Press, 2000), 70–92; and *Autobiography of Rear Admiral Charles Wilkes, U.S. Navy 1798–1877*, ed. William James Morgan, et al. (Washington, D.C.: Naval History Division, 1978), 321–65.

[9] Edward Troughton, along with business partner William Simms, built a three-foot diameter theodolite for the Coast Survey; previously, the survey had only possessed a two-foot diameter version of the instrument. For more on this device, see Hassler, *Principal Documents Relating to the Survey of the Coast*, 103–7.

determining the readings on the limb—[10]

On this occasion heliotropes were first used in this country in the Survey instead of Tin cones,—and their points of glitter[ing] light were visible by the naked eye from stations 30 or 40 miles distant—[11]

1837

Winter at Office in Washn.—bringing up the field work of the summer—Mr. Hassler conferred on J A. D. the appointment of 2^d^ Assist. in the Survey and charge of a party of Triangulation—He was and is the only Naval Officer that held such an appointment—their duty on the Survey being the Hydrographic—March 8th J A. D. was promoted to be a Lieutenant in the Navy—and soon after left Washington for the field—

But nearly four years of unceasing labor was beginning to tell upon eyes of uncommon power—so that by the time summer had arrived it was necessary to consult med. aid—and entire cessation from use of eyes was directed—

There was no remedy—just as the point of so much exertion was reached this terrible disaster intervened—

The active, hardy life in the field and the study of the closet must be relinquished—for weary hours without employment of any kind except to receive and follow the treatment of the Surgeons—

This continued until the fall without any apparent effect on the disease—the celebrated Oculist in Paris (Sichel) was suggested—and in Nov. J A. D left the U.S—arrived in Paris middle of Decem remained during the Winter and Spring—Eyes much benefitted by Sichel's treatment—[12]

1838

Not idle in Paris—observant of Professional novelties—About this time Paixhans was endeavoring to draw attention of French government to his system—J A. D.

10 In these segments, Dahlgren references plane surveying. This method relies on measures of distance and angles, from which triangulation can be used to compute other distances. "Readings on the limb" refers to the method of measuring angles in degrees; the vernier provided a finer measurement of that angle.

11 Both tin cones and heliotropes served as targets for measuring distances while surveying. The heliotrope reflected sunlight and thus served as a more readily visible target.

12 Treatment in Philadelphia had not been successful, so Dahlgren sought the care of Julius Sichel. Dahlgren believed his eyes had been injured by the long hours and fine detail required for the Coast Survey. A Navy surgeon declared that Dahlgren's optic nerves had been damaged. Robert J. Schneller Jr., *A Quest for Glory: A Biography of Rear Admiral John A. Dahlgren* (Annapolis: Naval Institute Press, 1996), 33–34.

translated his pamphlet and had it printed at his own expense for circulation in the Navy—[13]

In Octr. J A D. sent copy to Board of Commissioners—and received the usual official reply—All that was done was to fall into the traces of English & French precedent and as a consequence the U.S Navy was presented with tolerable copies of foreign ordnance—which it cost years of toil and contention to get rid of—[14]

1839

In January J A D. became a married man and retired for a season to recruit sight and health in the country—for two years this course was pursued rigorously—and to it is due the subsequent use of sight—not a word was read in writing or printing for two years and the ordinary work of the farm served for exercise—[15]

At the earliest moment Lieut. D. appeared for duty and was detailed for the Receiving ship at Philad—and in 1843 felt in condition to ask for sea-service—which obliged him to relinquish residence in the country and place his little family more conveniently—numbering three children one of whom was Ulric Dahlgren, who afterwards gave his life to his country—[16]

1843

So in 1843—Lt. D. went to sea in the frigate *Cumberland* bound to the Mediterranean—with the broad pendant of Commodore (now Admiral) Jos. Smith—one of the Navy's best officers—[17]

The cruise passed as usual in traversing the Med.—visiting its various ports, and supervising our affairs—this was the first cruise of the ship,—afterwards

[13] Henri Joseph Paixhans's system involved explosive shells. Schneller, *A Quest for Glory*, 33–34. The pamphlet was entitled *An Account of the Experiments Made in the French Navy for the Trial of Bomb Cannon, etc. By H. J. Paixhans, Lieut. Colonel of Artillery*. Philadelphia: E. G. Dorsey, 1838.

[14] Dahlgren advocated the use of shell-guns and the standardization of shipboard ordnance. These recommendations, advanced by Paixhans and later Dahlgren, were not adopted by the U.S. Navy for some time. Schneller, *A Quest for Glory*, 57–60.

[15] On 8 January 1839, Dahlgren married Mary C. Bunker. Following the advice of Dr. Thomas Harris, the new couple purchased a farm in Bucks County, PA. Dahlgren, *Memoir of John A. Dahlgren*, 78–79.

[16] Dahlgren's three children born at the farm were Charles Bunker, born in 1839; Elisabeth, born in 1840; and Ulric, born in 1842. Dahlgren, *Memoir of John A. Dahlgren*, 80.

[17] Commodore Joseph Smith commanded the Mediterranean Squadron.

Cumberland at the time of the Civil War. Drawing on paper; Alfred R. Waud, 1861.

Morgan collection of Civil War drawings, Library of Congress, Prints and Photographs Division, LC-DIG-ppmsca-21375.

she was sunk by the rebel "*Merrimac*"[18]—four of her officers afterwards became Admirals Commodore Smith—Captain Breese, Lieut. Foote and Lieut. D.[19]—Foote was the 1st Lieut. and exhibited the same energy and ability that afterwards marked his career before the country—the friendship begun between him and Lieut. D. endured for 20 years, until the latter stood by his death bed and listened to his name, among the last words uttered by the unconscious sufferer—during the whole of that period of 20 years time the utmost intimacy existed undisturbed by the slightest appearance of misunderstanding.

1845

The prospect of War with Mexico induced the return of the *Cumberland* in Decemr.—Soon afterwards Lieut. D. was assigned to Ordnance duty—during the war with Mexico he applied for sea-service there, but the Depart preferred to retain him where he was, for the introduction of novel means of warfare such as shells, war-rockets &c was rendering the ordnance duty of prime importance.

[18] On 8 March 1862, CSS *Virginia*, built on the remains of *Merrimack*, sank *Cumberland.*

[19] Smith and Samuel L. Breese received promotions to rear admiral on the retired list in 1862. Andrew Hull Foote and Dahlgren both received promotion to rear admiral during the Civil War while on active service.

CHAPTER 2

Ordnance Development to the Civil War, 1847–1860

1847

Commencement of career in the Ordnance by orders (Jan. 8th) for special duty at Washington—proved to be the charge of "Rocket Department"—then about to be introduced—The US had just purchased the right for $10,000[1]—Mason, Secretary of Navy an amiable & able man—[2] Commo. Warrington Chief of Bureau of Ordnance—a fine old sea-officer—remarkable for fine natural capacity—had captured An English vessel of War in 1814—stranger to me—[3] At that time the only trace of the present extensive establishment was the small Naval Laboratory under Mr Coston—[4]A new system of Armament the 32 pdr. unit-system was being introduced into our Navy, and the Locks, sights—fuses for shells were just beginning to be manufactured and these were scattered about in the differ-

1 The Hale rocket, a British design named after its inventor that used spin to stabilize it in flight, unlike a Congreve rocket, which relied upon a wooden stick. Dahlgren, Madeleine Vinton Dahlgren, *Memoir of John A. Dahlgren: Rear-Admiral United States Navy* (Boston: James R. Osgood and Company, 1882), 125–26; Taylor Peck, *Round-Shot to Rockets: A History of the Washington Navy Yard and U.S. Naval Gun Factory* (Annapolis, MD: United States Naval Institute, 1949), 105.

2 John Y. Mason (D-VA) served as Secretary of the Navy from March 1844 to March 1845 and again from September 1846 to March 1849.

3 Commo. Lewis Warrington, as master commandant, had captured the British brig *Epervier* during the War of 1812. When the bureau system was initiated in 1842, Warrington was placed in charge of the Bureau of Navy-Yards and Docks. He also oversaw the Bureau of Ordnance from 1846–1851. Charles Oscar Paullin, *Paullin's History of Naval Administration 1775–1911: A Collection of Articles from the U.S. Naval Institute* Proceedings (Annapolis, MD: U.S. Naval Institute, 1968), 210, 213.

4 B. Franklin Coston. Coston also oversaw the production of the Hale rockets. Martha J. Coston, *A Signal Success: The Work and Travels of Mrs. Martha J. Coston: An Autobiography* (Philadelphia: J. B. Lippincott, 1886), 24.

Commodore Lewis Warrington. Oil portrait, Rembrandt Peale, n.d.

Naval History and Heritage Command, Photographic Collections, NH119400.

ent workshops, chiefly in the Plumbers Dep:—Though not the first appliance was on hand for the manufacture of the rockets, a lot of them was prepared and dispatched in six or seven weeks for service in the fleet off the Mexican coast—Observing the want of system in Ordnance work I proposed a plan for collecting the scattered parts together into one Department—which was approved by the Bureau—and I was directed to take charge of the matter—No time to be lost in putting up larger buildings, I only asked to have the ship-timber cleared out of one end of a timber shed and a small quantity of machinery set up with the peculiar Ordn. appliances with all the effort that could be applied it was towards the close of the year that this first Ordn. workshop was ready for operations—Its scale could hardly have been more limited—but well did it serve its purpose for seven years—[5] and within its narrow limits was devised the present Armament of the Navy and the great establishment that chiefly supplied the Navy in the late war

When I first went to the Navy Yard a room was given me to write in, but I was not allowed a writer for some time and then just such a one as would offer for the smallest pittance

In this new building, there was still but one room for myself, the writer and another officer my assistant But the field was ample it was almost untouched, and my will was good—the form of things was not material—The Laboratory now devolved on me, for Mr Coston had left—a most able pyrotechnist and of much

[5] The Bureau of Ordnance approved Dahlgren's plan for a new ordnance workshop on 8 April 1847. The replacement ordnance building was completed on 8 May 1854. Peck, *Round-Shot to Rockets*, 105–6.

genius—it was a great loss—[6]

The work grew rapidly,—faster than the means—the new 32pdrs-were to be sighted—the ranges of all were needed—not one of which had been ascertained—therefore this was to be the first work—the usual mode of performing it—by firing on a piece of smooth ground was not to be found anywhere about—what could be substituted?—there was nothing but the sheet of water offered by the river—but such an experiment for accurate results had never been tried, and means were to be devised by which the jet of water could be determined with precision—this jet is thrown up by the shot when it strikes the water—and its duration is only for a few seconds—The Plane table would answer if a proper alidade could be invented suitable for such a rapid operation:—and this I must first devise.—it was done—then the points where this instrument was placed must be fixed with accuracy—which was done—A Base was measured—a series of Main triangles established,—the angles measured the results of imperfect means skewed our error of only one inch & a third[7]—In this I had no assistance save that of an excellent mechanic Mr John Holroyd to whom all these things were an entire novelty, but whose rapid perception and hearty zeal served me well—especially in the first service with the "Plane table"

1848

The full account is given in my Report to the Bureau—And printed by its order—[8]

The practice was intended to ascertain the ranges of the new 32 pdrs. just being introduced into the our Navy by recommendation of A Board of Officers

[6] Dahlgren has somewhat softened events here. He and Coston came into conflict over authority, and Warrington settled the dispute in favor of Dahlgren. According to his wife, Coston also developed a percussion primer on his own time, and an agreement he struck with the Navy fell through, leaving Coston embittered. Coston's wife also thought that Dahlgren had used the primer design in the Dahlgren gun without compensation. Coston, *A Signal Success*, 24–27; 298–99.

[7] An alidade is an instrument that can be used to measure both distance and angles; when used with the plane table, it facilitates surveying. The Washington Navy Yard lacked enough flat ground to test experimental guns; as noted, Dahlgren devised the above system in order to use the Anacostia River as a test range. Peck, *Round-Shot to Rockets*, 105; Dahlgren, *Memoir of John A. Dahlgren*, 128.

[8] John A. Dahlgren, *Report on the Thirty-two Pounder of Thirty-two cwt. to Commodore Warrington, Chief of the Bureau of Ordnance and Hydrography, by Lieut. Jno. A. Dahlgren* (Washington, DC: C. Alexander, 1850).

in 1845[9]—The object of it was to have but one calibre of gun and therefore one size of shot in all the ships, thereby avoiding the mistakes apt to occur in action, where so many pieces were to be supplied and so rapidly—This was a good object but the Board made a mistake in carrying it out—by adapting the 32 pdr. as the unit calibre—because we had then the 42 pdr. in service[10] which was better because it was more powerful—By taking the 32 pdr as the unit, they sacrificed the best guns in the service—They should have taken the 42 pdr. or even higher as the unit calibre—But they unluckily persuaded by the example of the English Navy which had just adopted the 32 pdr unit-calibre — they not only did this but they copied the weights and the models of the guns, so that our system became an imitation of the English—so we actually retrograded—It was this system that I finally overthrew after a struggle of seven or eight years, and for the 32pdrs & 8" shell guns gave the Navy my IX^{inch} and XI^{inch} Guns—firing shells of 72^{lbs} and 130^{lbs}—and shot of 96^{lbs} and 170^{lbs}—It was the XI^{in} guns of the *Kearsarge* that beat the best English Guns on the *Alabama* and vindicated my theory—[11]

The ranges were to furnish the means of adjusting & graduating sights to the new 32 pdrs—When one gun (a light 32pdr) had been so fitted, the Chief of Ordnance, Commodore Warrington came down to have occular proof of the merit of the new sights—the firing cut out the water-line of a target, and so convinced the gallant old Warrior that he gave orders forthwith substituting the new sights for the old disparts[12]—the tools of his own day—with which he had captured a British vessel of War (*Epervier*)—

This subject however important had not monopolised my attention The Navy was entirely destitute of Boat Guns—occasionally an old carronade—or a field piece from the army had appeared as such in great necessity—but they were so useless in boats as never to be used at this time and we were without any proper

9 Secretary of the Navy Mason appointed a board to evaluate the state of the Navy's ordnance in 1845. The board recommended improvements in the quality of manufactured guns, better standardization of training, the use of shells, and the use of a 32-pounder gun on the British model. Robert J. Schneller Jr., *A Quest for Glory: A Biography of Rear Admiral John A. Dahlgren* (Annapolis, MD: Naval Institute Press, 1996), 69–72.

10 JAD: "See Shells & Shell-Guns 273 &c." John A. Dahlgren, *Shells and Shell Guns* (Philadelphia: King and Baird, 1856), 273.

11 On 19 June 1864, the Confederate screw-sloop *Alabama* fought *Kearsarge* off Cherbourg, France. As Dahlgren noted, *Kearsarge* mounted Dahlgren guns while *Alabama* did not.

12 A dispart is a marking or piece of metal at the muzzle that allows the gun to be aimed parallel to the axis of the bore. [William Falconer,] *A New Universal Dictionary of the Marine*..., ed. William Burney (London: Joyce Gold, 1815), 124.

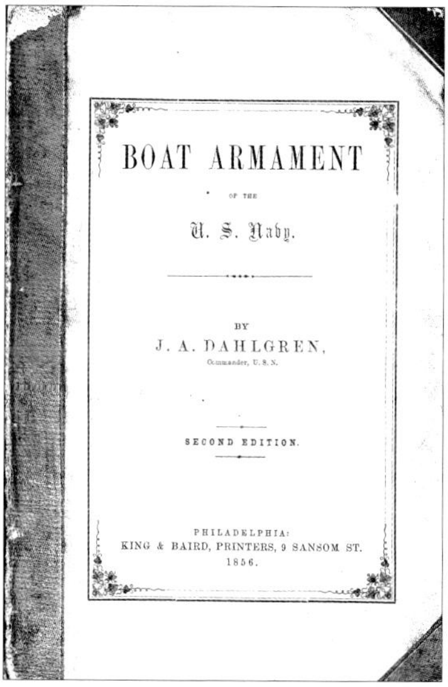
BOAT ARMAMENT

OF THE

U. S. Navy.

BY

J. A. DAHLGREN,

Commander, U. S. N.

SECOND EDITION.

PHILADELPHIA:

KING & BAIRD, PRINTERS, 9 SANSOM ST.

1856.

A presentation copy of the second edition of *Boat Armament of the U.S. Navy.*

Naval History and Heritage Command, Navy Department Library.

Naval light artillery—

In the spring of this year I had submitted a system of Howitzer Boat Armament to the Bureau, with a model of a Howitzer, and asked leave with such means as were at hand to prosecute the matter—opinions about the Bureau were not favorable to me—and the leave asked was only given at this time, when the Chief began to see reason for confidence in my views—

So on the very day that he witnessed the practice above alluded to, I was able to show him the casting of the first Howitzer—There was not a boring Lathe in the Yard, so this first gun was finished on an ordinary lathe having also been cast with the most primitive means—Neither myself nor a person about me—had ever seen a gun cast or finished—and it was also the first time that I had ever drafted or computed such—

Yet as good luck would have it the little gun answered perfectly—it required a peculiar carriage which I designed—and that also succeeded—The Chief came down to see its operations, and brought down others—the little gun was exhibited on early occasion to a large number of officers—passing well through every ordeal and establishing the initiative from which the present extensive system of Boat Howitzers dates—(A full account of it is given in the work "System of Boat Armament 1st & 2nd Editions—1852 & 1856)[13]

The opposition did not cease here but tried to turn me by flank movement—which utterly failed—I advanced step by step until the whole system was completely introduced into Naval service—light & heavy bronze 12 pdrs and 24 pdrs—with Boat and Field carriages—perfect in every detail—An order of the Navy Department Dec. 17. 1850[14] recognized this system and directed full com-

[13] J[ohn] A. Dahlgren, *A System of Boat Armament in the United States Navy: Reported to Commodore Charles Morris* (Philadelphia: A. Hart, 1852) and J[ohn] A. Dahlgren, *Boat Armament of the U.S. Navy*, 2nd ed. (Philadelphia: King and Baird, 1856).

[14] JAD: "See Boat Arm 2d Edition page 21." Secretary of the Navy William A. Graham issued an order with specifications and standards for boat armament.

pliance with it—

A service of 12 years in peace and four years in War (1861 to 1865) has fully confirmed the theory and the execution of my system—it remains now unaltered in either from the first designs—

1849

In this year the plan of collecting and organising the Ordnance work in the Navy Yard (Wash$^{n.}$) into a whole—proceeded—machinery was purchased from time to time and put up in the little apartment assigned to it—The character and style of the Boat Howitzers had been fixed and the manufacture for service was begun—The first ever issued was sent to the "*Adams*" June 1849—[15]

Various supplies of Ordnance equipment began to issue to all the other Yards—

My attention had however been seriously given to a more important object—The armament of our Ships as decided by the Board of 1845 was entirely against my convictions,—it had been a step to the rear and was not only short of the true standard but inferior to the armament that it had superseded—it had not only excluded the more powerful 42 pdr—but introduced confusion into the Magazine while it simplified the shot locker—

I was aware that I could do nothing towards curing this evil, unless well backed by influence—the opinion of the Navy would not supply this, for the authorities who represented that opinion had recently decided on the unit-calibre of the 32 pdr—my own experience would not give the influence, for that was too limited as yet,—so I resolved to amass such a body of well arranged facts as would furnish the influence

So I quietly watched each days practice and jotted down facts as they appeared—these escaped even the notice of those who looked upon every step in my proceeding—At last one them was of a character not to be overlooked, and excited an alarm which assisted well in hastening the period when my views might be expounded without fear of being laughed at

It is true that this fact nearly cost me my life and did kill a warrant officer close by me—but it was worth more than it cost—

On the 13th Nov. 1849 while firing a new heavy 32 pdr, it burst & killed the Gunner—a portion of the breech weighing 2000^{lbs} tore up the ground a foot from me—[16]

[15] The first howitzer was sent to *John Adams* on 6 June 1849. Peck, *Round-Shot to Rockets*, 106.

[16] In margin, JAD: "his birth day."

A few weeks previously I had opened the question with the Chief, in conversing with him on the results of the new 32 pdr. system, by saying that "its most powerful guns lacked accuracy, and its accurate guns lacked power"—The veteran asked me to explain—which I did in a very few words—to his demand what would I do,—I replied by asking leave to submit the draft of a new gun—The bursting of the 32 pdr. gave an influence to my statements which perhaps nothing else could have done—[17]

With a hopeful heart I sat down to compute & draft a gun—it was the IX inch shell-gun[18]—

1850

The draft of the IXinch gun was submitted early in the year—and an order given at once for casting one of the kind—

In May 1850, I had the satisfaction of seeing the first piece laid on the wharf of the Navy Yard—fearful that opinion was not yet ripe for such a innovation as a battery solely of shell-guns I had drafted a 50 pdr. to fall back upon— and this came with the IXinch

Before these arrivals I had used an opportunity to sketch my views more into a shape[19]—The Chairman of the Senate's Naval Committee looking about for some information that might guide legislative action in regard to the construction of War Steamers, had addressed me a letter (Febr. 25) upon the subject—In discussing it (Mar. 19) I sketched a large propeller frigate that should be armed with the heavy cannon which I had in hand—going as far as I considered safe in trenching upon old ideas—[20]

The first practice with the new IXinch so fully confirmed my views, that I was enabled to abate nothing whatever of them,—but to adhere to my notions in full—and to ask for the casting of an XIinch gun which the Chief promptly

---

17 Dahlgren, after the accident, made a report to Warrington that detailed a number of bursting guns aboard U.S. vessels. He concluded that "the great importance of heavy ordnance to a navy, is evident from its being its chief dependence, and too much care and expense can hardly be given to its improvement, so that neither the fate of a ship, nor the lives of men, may be jeopardized by the bursting of a gun." Dahlgren, *Memoir of John A. Dahlgren*, 135.

18 At foot of page, JAD: "Much of this he did at home 4½ street rising betimes & working till time to go to the yard."

19 In margin, JAD: "This year published my first work on Ordnance being Report on "Practice with 32 pdr." See Dahlgren, *Report on the Thirty-two Pounder*.

20 Dahlgren had received letters from the chairman of the Senate Naval Affairs Committee, David L. Yulee. In response, Dahlgren offered suggestions on new types of ships and advocated for heavier guns, among other points. Schneller, *A Quest for Glory*, 99–100.

assented—so well satisfied was he of my proceedings—for which he was entitled to much credit, for opinion was adverse almost without exception—the strange form of the cannon, seemed uncouth to eyes which had been accustomed to the more graceful form of those adopted by all countries while the weights of cannon and projectile seemed a unwieldly exaggeration—the great heresy of introducing an entire battery of shell guns, appeared monstrous when the most enterprising advocates here and abroad would venture no further than two or four 8^inch guns in any one ship

But the veteran chief as he once said to me "never gave his confidence by halves" So an XI^inch gun was ordered and he just lived to know of its completion—for on the 15. Septr 1851 the gallant Warrior[21] was seized with a mortal disease, though to all appearance in the enjoyment of his usual robust health, and died in less than a month (12th Octr—)

No one had more reason to lament his loss than myself—it postponed the fulfilment of my plans for several years—Among his last acts was to approve my plans for a building suitable for the extent which the Ordnance work of the Yard began to assume—and which is now used for that purpose—

In this year Congress called upon the Secr. of War (Conrad) for his views in regard to Coast defences[22]—to make which more, complete he called on some officers of Army and Navy—among them—Commos. Morris and Perry—Dupont—Maury of the Observatory—De Russey, Chase and Delafield of the Engineers—myself also[23]—That of Perry was remarkable because he advocated

21 At bottom, JAD: "Warrington."

22 At the request of the House of Representatives, Secretary of War Charles M. Conrad undertook a survey of the coastal defenses of the United States and to evaluate the system of defenses planned in 1816. "Letter from the Secretary of War in Reference to Fortifications," 11 December 1851. 32d Congress, 1st Session, House Executive Document No. 5, 1-2.

23 After a lengthy summary of fortifications from Chief of Engineers Joseph G. Totten, the views of the following naval officers appeared in the report submitted to the House of Representatives: Commo. Charles Morris, Commo. Matthew C. Perry, Cmdr. Robert B. Cunningham, Cmdr. Samuel Francis Du Pont, Lt. Joseph Lanman, Lt. Matthew Fontaine Maury, and Lt. John A. Dahlgren (though his name appears as "I. A. Dahlgreen"). Lt. Col. René Edward De Russy, Maj. William H. Chase, and Maj. Richard Delafield provided the views of the Army.

the use of Steam Rams—the next to do so, after Commo Barron,[24] who earnestly urged the idea perhaps 20 years before, and whose model stood for some time in the Rotunda of the Capitol—the butt for cavils and sneers—Dupont's paper was also written with his usual ability—My own paper was lengthy, and was used to introduce my plan of armament for ships of War—exemplified on a Screw frigate carrying IX^inch^ guns on the gun Deck and Pivot X^inch^ or XI^in^ guns on the Spar Deck, all shell guns but to be capable of firing shot if necessary This Document with all the papers was printed by order of Congress—(32^d^ Congress 1st Session Ex. Doc. No. 5) and also in 1862—37. Congress 2^d^ Session Report No. 86

1852

These public statements together with the practical results themselves gradually familiarised the public & the Navy with the idea of the change proposed—And so far that in 1852, the attention of the Chairman of the Naval Committee (Mr. Stanton[25]) was drawn to the subject and he entered on its consideration with ability and vigor—In order to have a full detail of the plan proposed he addressed a formal request in August (1852) to the Bureau of Ordnance for my views—to which I replied at length and advised the construction of a new screw frigate suitable for the guns proposed—IX^inch^ & XI^inch^

On the 17th Aug. Mr. Stanton, by instruction of the Naval Committee, moved for an appropriation for this purpose, and supported it by a most able exposition and argument, in which he cited parts of my paper—the effort nearly succeeded,—but there was too much novelty in the idea—it met with the opposition of the Navy Department & some of the Bureaus—therefore failed—but only for a season—[26]

This year my work on Boat Armament was published explaining the System of Howitzers which I had devised, and which was rapidly taking its place in our

[24] Commo. James Barron had written a treatise on steam tactics in 1832. John S. C. Abbott, "Charles Ellet and His Naval Steam Rams," *Harper's New Monthly Magazine* No. 189 (February 1866): 299. In his paper, Perry remarked that extensive fortifications were both expensive and ineffective and that an enemy could easily blockade a port at some distance. Because of this, Perry advocated the use of steamers of war to mount an active defense. He declared that "I cannot entertain the idea that we are always to act on the defensive; on the contrary, it is more reasonable to suppose that, in the event of another war, the power of the United States will be felt beyond their own immediate coasts; most certainly it ought to be, for we have the means of placing ourselves upon an equality of naval strength with any of the European nations." "Letter from the Secretary of War in Reference to Fortifications," 140.

[25] Frederick P. Stanton (D-TN).

[26] Commo. Charles Morris, who took charge of the Bureau of Ordnance, likely led the opposition to Dahlgren's proposal. Schneller, *A Quest for Glory*, 107–11.

ships—(this was the second work on Ordnance)[27]

1853

This year was passed in maturing ideas,—collecting facts—putting up the present Ordnance building—Meeting the demands of the service for Howitzers—practising with the XI^inch gun &c—The Bureau would not however encourage the new Cannon—and they remained at a stand—I missed my old friend Commo. Warrington—

This year appeared my third work on Ordnance—on "Percussion Primers and Locks"—explaining some novelties going into service[28]

1854

—Was to mark a new era in the progress of the Navy—The "*Merrimac*" class of ships date at this time—[29]The pressure of the day demanded change, the fine sailing frigates of 1820 needed steam,—and the few steamers we had were not frigates—So a class of frigate was designed, being in plan, that which Mr Stanton would have authorised two years ago and the appropriation obtained—When the armament was discussed, it was found that the regulation Cannon the 32 pdr of the service would not answer—The ships were to be 3000 tons, one half greater than the largest ever built and as large as a 74—but having only two decks would carry but 60 guns—so large a ship with 60—32 pdrs was rediculous—So there was no escape from my proposition, reiterated so often in three years—the guns were queer looking things to be sure,—one facetious old gentleman of past ideas called them "tadpoles" one day and asked how they got on—I replied that they would be full grown frogs in good time—but queer as they looked, they have beat every other gun put alongside of them—So it was decided to place IX^inch guns on the Main deck—that was a great step—but to place XI^inch above, that would never do—it must await another time:—but I was told that if I would draft a X^inch gun on my model, it should be carried as a chase gun, one at each end—which will account for the existence of this gun—the rest of the guns on the spar deck were to be 8^inch guns—I protested against these liberties with my

27 Dahlgren, *A System of Boat Armament in the United States Navy.*

28 John A. Dahlgren, *Naval Percussion Locks and Primers, Particularly Those of the United States* (Philadelphia: A. Hart, 1853).

29 The appropriation provided for six steam vessels. The *Merrimack* class consisted of the steam frigates *Merrimack, Wabash, Minnesota, Colorado,* and *Roanoke*. The sixth vessel was the steam sloop *Niagara*. Paul H. Silverstone, *Civil War Navies* 1855–1883 (Annapolis, MD: Naval Institute Press, 2001), 15, 17.

plan, but it was of no weight—Mr. Secretary Dobbin by way of compensation, told me I should arm the vessel that was to be built by Mr. Steers—[30]and towards the end of July brought us together—but Mr Steers had unfortunately undertaken to fix one of the principal conditions of Armament that his vessel, the *Niagara*—was only to carry cannon on the Spar deck—and he had gone too far to make any change though persuaded by me of the propriety—So in this way my plan was cut in two—the *Merrimac* had my main deck battery and the *Niagara* my spar deck battery—and thus the plan like a circus rider rode the ring with a foot on each horse—

1855

To the usual Ordn. business was added all the labor of superintending the fabrication of so many new guns at different foundries—for there to be six new screw frigates—Steers and myself too had much to arrange, until one day an accident deprived him of life I had received a letter from him and soon afterwards was telegraphed that he was thrown from his carriage:—

His death was a national misfortune—much intercourse with him showed me a man without ordinary education but the want of it could not restrain his fine native powers—He would have been the greatest shipbuilder of the time—

In the midst of the anxieties comes the great sorrow, in the departure from this life of the mother of my children—then five—all in fine health & promising the third was Ulric[31]

In the fall I am promoted to be a Commander[32]

1856

In January dies Commodore Morris Chief of Bureau of Ordnance—a distinguished and excellent officer—When this occurred the Secr. of Navy sent for me and said that the President intended to make me Chief of Bur. Of Ordnance, but

---

30 James Cochrane Dobbin served as Secretary of the Navy from March 1853 to March 1857. George Steers was constructor for *Niagara*.

31 Dahlgren's wife died in June 1855. Beyond the children mentioned earlier, they also had John, who died in infancy in 1844; Paul, born on 9 August 1846; Eva, born on 19 March 1848; and Lawrence, born on 12 November 1850, who also died in infancy. Dahlgren, *Memoir of John A. Dahlgren*, 98, 123; and Schneller, *A Quest for Glory*, 133–34.

32 Dahlgren's was promoted on 14 September 1855. Edward W. Callahan, ed., *List of Officers of the Navy of the United States and of the Marine Corps from 1775 to 1900: Comprising a Complete Register of All Present and Former Commissioned, Warranted, and Appointed Officers of the United States Navy, and of the Marine Corps, Regular and Volunteer* (New York: L. R. Hammersly & Co., 1901), 146.

that the law required one to be a Captain, while I was only a Commander, but that he thought of postponing the appointment until law could be amended—I preferred that the effort should not be made

This year was published my fourth Ordn. work—"Second edition of Boat Armament" and at the end of the year my fifth & principal work "Shells & Shell Guns"—designed to illustrate some of the points of my theory—it was inscribed to my friend Foote—(afterwards Admiral)[33]

1857

It now became necessary for me to go to sea—the strongest point of my system was strenuously resisted and could get no foothold on ship board—the officers believed it unmanageable at sea & impracticable—So after much solicitation—by me and opposition from men who should not have done so, I obtained command of the *Plymouth*, a fine sloop of War with full leave to alter & arrange at my pleasure—one of the redoubtable XI^{inch} guns that a frigate was not supposed able to carry was mounted on the *Plymouth* and I proceeded to sea—[34]

As the training of seamen to serve as Gun-Captains was an essential to the proper use of the Battery I undertook to make the *Plymouth* a Gunnery ship—and to relieve the monotony of ship life, a cruise was made along the European Coast—first touched Fayal, then at Lisbon England & Holland—here I visited the Royal foundries at Liege—also visited the British Navy Yard—and was well received—went on board the *Excellent*,—celebrated as the English Gunnery ship—also the *Diadem*, a new screw Frigate intended to match our *Merrimac*—for as soon as the *M.* had been completed, she was sent to England to show what we could do, and as a consequence in less than a twelve-month they had several frigates even larger in course of construction and the *Diadem*, one of them, was ready for trial—it so happened that I was on board during the trial trip[35]

On my return I had the satisfaction of reporting that the XI^{inch} was entirely manageable at sea—and so disappeared the last objection to the system—and soon after they took place in the arming of our vessels, particularly the new

---

[33] Dahlgren, *Boat Armament in the United States Navy*, 2nd ed.

[34] *Plymouth* functioned as a kind of test-bed for Dahlgren's system of ship armament; the Navy referred to it as a "gunnery practice ship." The XI-inch gun was widely supposed to be too heavy to go to sea. Dahlgren, *Memoir of John A. Dahlgren*, 185–86.

[35] Secretary of the Navy Isaac Toucey instructed Dahlgren to travel to the Azores, Portugal, France, Holland, England, and Bermuda. He added, "You are authorized to visit the most important arsenals of the different countries at which you may touch." While in England, Dahlgren witnessed the first trial of the English screw-frigate *Diadem* on 2 October 1857. Ibid., 192, 199.

gunboats—The winter passed with the usual round of Ordnance duty and in the Spring the *Plymouth* was again ready for sea—

Just then came the tidings that the British cruisers were taking unwarrantable liberties with our merchant vessels passing near Cuba—I volunteered to the service of the *Plymouth*, for she was in fine fighting order—and urged it—The Secr. of the Navy[36] consented—and the *Plymouth* was ordered to the spot to join the other vessels sent on the same duty—The English commander acted a wise part, he immediately stopped the practice and sent away the vessels which had been engaged in it—[37]

This over, the *Plymouth* & *Saratoga* sailed for Port au Prince to settle a difficulty about the Grand Island of Nevassa[38]—thence the *Plymouth* sailed for San Juan—and from that port to Vera Cruz to convey our Minister[39] to the U.S — While awaiting his arrival from the city of Mexico, I received a dispatch from our Consul (Mr Chase)[40] at Tampico, urging the presence of the *Plymouth* to put a stop to sundry outrages on American citizens—having no orders I took the responsibility and went to Tampico—where I had an interview with Gen. Garza[41] and required redress for what he had done—he promised to abstain from such proceedings in future, but would not or could not disgorge the property seized: So I repaired to Vera Cruz and had an interview with President Juarez on the subject—it is pleasant to say that he listened attentively to my presentation of the several offences committed by Garza and in each case answered that my demand should be complied with—which was truly & promptly done as said—and I received the thanks of the merchants concerned—for the merchandize recovered was of value—(mentioned in Annual Report of Navy Department

---

36 Isaac Toucey served as secretary of the Navy from 7 March 1857 to 6 March 1861.

37 The British ships had been stopping American vessels to interdict the slave trade; Schneller, *A Quest for Glory*, 160.

38 Americans had been taking guano, for use as fertilizer, from Nevassa. Haitian vessels had ejected the American citizens, and Commander Thomas Turner, in command of *Saratoga*, went to Port-au-Prince to make American dissatisfaction known. *Report of the Secretary of the Navy* 1858, 14–15.

39 John Forsyth Jr.

40 U.S. Consul Franklin Chase.

41 Gen. Juan José de la Garza was governor of Tamaulipas.

Dec. 6. 1858)[42] After landing our Minister at Mobile the *Plymouth* proceeded on her way to Washington, and arrived there early in the winter—About this time the new screw Sloops of War of the *Brooklyn* class[43] were building as well as the Screw Gunboats—and the XI^inch at last took its place on board of most of them—for the experience in the *Plymouth* had entirely dissipated the last signs of opposition; and thus the Armament that was to carry the National vessels through the terrible ordeal of Civil War was finally triumphant, after a struggle of Six or seven years—the old school argued against them and the British rediculed them with such slang as "Soda water bottles" which in some measure resembled but they weathered opposition and do still.

1859

This year was passed in various labors in Ordnance—chiefly of administration—Only one progressive measure was proposed by me and was adopted—the building of a large Foundry suitable for conducting some of the Experimental work which I preferred to keep under my own eye—The designs of the interior were my own—the architectural designs were by the Draftsman of the Ordnance draftsman Mr. Cluss[44]

The armament of the Navy had scarcely been firmly established when symptoms of being superseded by a rival began to loom up—in various rifled Cannon but chiefly that devised by Armstrong—and the drift of opinion military Naval and Civil set decidedly towards the new Comer—the reports that came across the water by every mail were all of a color—and threatened to sweep away all I had built up without even discussion—The question was a serious one for me in one respect, but it was of much greater importance to the country that for the sake of a personal interest I should not stand in the way of a real improvement—and at that time my position fully enabled me to do so—it was not the first time I had considered the subject,—in 1856 it was noticed at some length in my work on "Shells and Shell Guns"—the muzzle loader of Lancaster had been tried, and the Breech loading cannon of Cavalli had given results in range & accuracy not sur-

[42] Garza had been forcing American merchants to take loans. Chase and Dahlgren met with Garza "and remonstrated against his measures." Later they met with Mexican President Juarez and "obtained from him the assurance the proceedings complained of were contrary to regulations, and that no such levies would be enacted in the future." *Report of the Secretary of the Navy* 1858, 15.

[43] Actually the *Hartford* class, which consisted of *Hartford, Brooklyn, Lancaster, Pensacola,* and *Richmond.* Silverstone, *Civil War Navies*, 20–21.

[44] JAD: "since well known in Washington for the design of several Churches & public buildings." Adolf Cluss, who later became City Engineer of Washington, DC.

passed to this day—I had also been at the practice ground of Braschaet[45] in Belgium (1857) and had seen there very heavy rifle cannon and heard what they had done—But none of them had been able to satisfy the artillerists of the day—not even Cavalli's,—the best of them—and in its work not inferior to Armstrong's[46]

Investigation and results had not been confined to England but were going on in France, and had received a confirmation from actual service in the field, which imparted to them an interest equal to that created by the English gun—The rifle Cannon of the Emperor had made its debut at Magenta and seemed capable of all that could be desired—[47]

Subsequent experience has shown how dangerous it is to pass judgement on first facts—however decisive—particularly when official authorities[48] command the opinions of those who pass judgement,—or where powerful interests are involved—It may be said now, that neither the Armstrong gun nor the Emperor's rifle gun has sustained the reputation so easily won when they first appeared—

It was due to the interests in my charge to meet the feverish excitement of the day and to contribute something to the solution of the question—So during the summer I entered up its study and prepared drafts of an Iron and a Bronze rifled cannon—projectiles &c—both were cast in my own Department and in Septem. the Iron gun, a 40 pdr. had first trial and performed satisfactorily,—and soon after the Bronze rifle made its debut—it was designed to enter into the Boat Armament, and stood the test so well that it preserves its place there to this day—

1860

This year was chiefly devoted to the prosecution of the Rifle question,—in which I adhered to the views already explained,—nothing deterred by the brilliant results of the Armstrong gun—that my early judgement was not erroneous is best shown by the fact that Armstrong himself has abandoned the manufacture of breech loading Cannon of heavy Calibre, and has felt obliged to return to the

45 Brasschaat, Belgium, was home to a proving ground of the Royal Belgian Artillery.

46 Both the designs of Giovanni Cavalli and Charles William Lancaster were early rifled pieces. Lancaster guns saw service during the Crimean War, but proved prone to bursting and were removed from service. The Armstrong gun, of Sir William Armstrong, another British rifled breech-loader, was more successful, but it too proved fragile in the field. Spencer Tucker, *Arming the Fleet: U.S. Navy Ordnance in the Muzzle-Loading Era* (Annapolis, MD: Naval Institute Press, 1989), 225–26.

47 French forces under Emperor Napoleon III used a rifled cannon at the Battle of Magenta during the Second War of Italian Independence in 1859.

48 Before writing "official authorities," Dahlgren had written, and crossed out, both "a superior," and "a crowned head."

muzzle loader which thereby limits him merely to material for construction[49]

By the end of the year I was able to submit to the Bureau of Ordn. a satisfactory summary of results and to feel confident of having assured some steps in this difficult question—the Navy light artillery for instance received a rifle gun the 12 pdr—which after the test of continued war service may be considered as the established rifled Howitzer for Boats and for landing An iron 50 pdr. was also closely scrutinised and proved to be correct in the essential features—pitch of rifling, length of bore,—form of gun &c[50] and hence I arrived at the data for heavier cannon as far as the 150 pdr.—but a troublesome question remained, the character of metal suitable for endurance,—which I should have pursued, had it not been for the intervention of a more momentous question—

Above all the practice of the two years supplied me with facts to dispel the prevailing illusion as to the performance of rifle-cannon at fabulous distances—[51]

But as already said I was cut short in these enquiries by the looming up of a danger that menaced the country with destruction and compelled all of us to resist it with such means as we were possessed of—the best heads in the country had failed in the argument, and the cannon and bayonet were to be appealed to—So far as the Navy was concerned I had no misgivings in regard to the Ordnance with which I had supplied it—

In the last month of this year the State of So. Carolina seceded[52] and set an example which other states were not slow to follow—

The last important labor of this year was to draw the attention of the Depart. to the great importance of providing some ironclads for the Navy—I referred to the propositions which I had made in 1852, eight years before, on this subject—and reminded the Bureau of Ordn. that no notice had been taken of them—I now urged the matter once more,—by accident the letter found its way to Congress, instead of my report on rifled Cannon which had been called for, and was

---

49 JAD: "that is whether a gun shall be made of wrought iron or cast."

50 JAD: "See Congress. Doc.—Ex. Doc. No. 43—36th Congr. 2d Session." In "Rifled Cannon and the Armament of Ships-of-War," Dahlgren sent to Congress the results of trials with various kinds of naval ordnance and their results. 36th Congress, 2d Session, House of Representatives, Ex. Doc. No. 43.

51 During 1859 and 1860, as noted here, Dahlgren worked on evaluating rifled cannon. He found the concept to be sound, but thought, as indicated above, that a metal strong enough for a rifled piece remained to be found. During the Civil War, Dahlgren came to believe that rifled guns had failed to live up to their promise. Many rifled guns had burst during service and were seen as unreliable. The increased range failed to compensate for the sacrifice in reliability. Schneller, *A Quest for Glory*, 166–75, 345–56.

52 20 December 1860.

printed[53] but neither this nor my repeated personal solicitations to members of the Naval Committees were of any avail—the whole subject was ignored until the great necessities of the country compelled its consideration—It is needless for me to point out how sorely we were pressed afterwards and what risks were run from neglect of my entreaties—[54]

[53] JAD: "See Ex. Doc. No. 25 36th Congress. 2d Session." In his remarks, Dahlgren discussed shell guns and armor potential means of protecting against them. "A Report of the Superintendent of Ordnance of the Washington Navy Yard on Rifled Cannon and the Armament of Ships of War," 36th Congress, 2d Session, Executive Document 25.

[54] It was only under the threat of confronting Confederate ironclads that the United States Navy finally embarked on building some of its own. Dahlgren suggests here that had the Navy listened to his recommendations, they would have begun the Civil War already equipped with ironclads. Howard J. Fuller, *Clad in Iron: The American Civil War and the Challenge of British Naval Power* (Westport, CT: Praeger, 2008), 50–54.

CHAPTER 3

Outbreak and Early Years of the Civil War, 1861–62

1861

It has been the invariable custom of the Naval service to eschew all active participation in the politics of the day—a custom approved by people and rulers—and to which I have always conformed—

The question that presented itself to every American on the first day of this year was far removed from the sphere of ordinary politics,—though it had originated there:—The existence of the Union was threatened,—S.C. had already withdrawn—two of the Cabinet had resigned (Floyd & Cobb)—and all around, the signs of political dissolution were gathering—[1]

Placed where I was, these signs were daily before me in the working of the Federal Machinery, and I was in immediate contact with the actors the ideas which naturally arose were that no evils due solely to the management of the machine were to be cured by its destruction—one might as well commit suicide to cure a disease—moreover there was no right reserved to pursue such a course,—happily it proved there was not the power either—Yet the topic and no other was to be heard on all sides—In Congress and out—officers as well as citizens—

One very common practice was now found to work badly—to accommodate the officers of the Navy when on shore duty it was usual to assign them to the Navy Yards located in or nearest to the sections to which they belonged—so that most of the officers of the several Naval stations in the South were Southern officers—So it was at the Navy Yard Washington,—and I soon found that these gentlemen gradually receded from that frank communion which is apt to exist

[1] Secretary of War John B. Floyd, from Virginia, and Secretary of the Treasury Howell Cobb, from Georgia, had both resigned in December 1860.

between officers of the same service—there was naturally a strong southern sympathy among the residents of Washington,—for it is Southern soil—and thus I finally became conscious that my position was daily becoming isolated—[2]

In the first month of the year events seemed hastening rapidly to a conclusion—five more States withdrew[3]—Senators & Representatives were abandoning their seats—The last Southern man in the Cabinet resigned[4]—Military & Naval officers were doing the same—and the Flag of the Nation was even fired upon, in consequence of an attempt to relieve the handful of men that held Fort Sumter—There seemed to be no restraining hand to arrest the dissolution of the Country—The President officially declared that he [had] not the power of coercion—and there was obviously no other remedy—[5]

Upon this mournful spectacle I looked with sorrow & indignation—surely the great Nation should not thus and so early come to its end—

Now, there arose suppressed rumors that the Navy Yard would be seized by a mob,— ill-looking fellows whom no one knew, began to appear & cluster about the corners and places of resort—the police was not reliable, and the military force in the city nothing—The Ordnance Dept. of the Yard was filled with a stock of arms, not large but choice and a large amount of ammunition,—these were in my keeping and it behoved me to look to my charge—selecting the most defensible building I caused all the breech-loading rifles—and light artillery to be transferred thither,—in parcels so as to avoid notice,—all the windows were barricaded, and the doors, save two, which were commanded by two Howitzers,—a stove, fuel, and water were provided and on the pretext of some special work, no one was allowed to enter but a small body of seamen employed in the Ordnance, who I knew would obey my orders, whatever they were—As it would be unsafe to include the large quantity of powder, or to blow up the Yard magazines, I had it secretly carried into the Cock-loft of the large Ordnance workshops—

2 For more on the resignation of naval officers during the secession crisis and after, see: William S. Dudley, *Going South: U.S. Navy Officer Resignations & Dismissals on the Eve of the Civil War* (Washington, DC: Naval Historical Foundation, 1981).

3 Alabama, Mississippi, Florida, Georgia, and Louisiana.

4 Secretary of the Interior Jacob Thompson.

5 In his message to Congress on 3 December 1860, President James Buchanan stated that the executive lacked the power to coerce states. Buchanan sought to achieve a compromise with the Southern states, but as one prominent historian noted, there was "a general assumption that little of the enterprise and inspiration needed to save the Union could be expected from the White House . . . Buchanan's purpose, it transpired, was to avoid . . . extremes until the arrival of March 4 released him from his responsibilities." David M. Potter, *The Impending Crisis 1848–1861* (New York: Harper and Row, 1976), 517–21.

which was in range of my guns in the Shell House, and could be fired by shells if needed,—finally I sent all the spare money that belonged to me and had it deposited at Philad. for the use of my family—having done so it only remained to await and meet coming events—

The apprehension of violence and riot had also taken hold of the citizens—they felt that their families and property were in danger—so meetings were got up with the view of forming Companies of Volunteers—but the object seemed to be the repression of a mob—And the danger of attempts to seize the Capital seemed to attract official attention—for Congress ordered a Committee to enquire, while the Executive quietly drew in some companies of Regulars for the general security, though then with the Marines in the District barely amounted to 500 men

The alarm was by no means ill-founded for it was recognised that the various symptoms of disorder corresponded with the suggestion of a Richmond paper to seize Washington[6]—Meanwhile incendiarism began to occur too frequently, and night patrols of citizens were arranged to supply the obvious inefficiency of the police—

The month of February furnished its quota of exciting incident,—The insecurity of Wash: and the conviction that a sudden blow was meditated still weighed on the minds of all,—The Congressional Comm. were unable to obtain any evidence of a tangible character but the operations of a conspiracy seldom furnish that,—some thought the idea had been abandoned, but Gen. Scott[7] bluntly told the Comm. that there was "abundant evidence in his mind to justify him in making military preparations" to guard against such scheming and so he continued to draw in to the city such Regulars as were available—adding in this way about 400 men to the force in hand—this was distributed in the public buildings or in their vicinity—and by way of further precaution the vaults & cellars of the Capitol were examined every night[8]

---

[6] The particular paper and article are not known. Fears that Southerners would seize Washington circulated in the city after the election of Lincoln. For more on the suspected conspiracies, and investigations into them, see. David C. Keehn, *Knights of the Golden Circle: Secret Empire, Southern Secession, Civil War* (Baton Rouge: Louisiana State University Press, 2013), 100–12.

[7] Lt. Gen. Winfield Scott, who along with Congress, worked to ensure the defense of the District of Columbia. The committee mentioned here was likely the Committee of Arrangements, which bore responsibility for Abraham Lincoln's inauguration ceremonies. Winfield Scott, *Memoirs of Lieut.-General Winfield Scott*, ed. Timothy D. Johnson (1864; repr., Knoxville: University of Tennessee Press, 2015), 309.

[8] Federal authorities apparently feared that Confederate saboteurs would place explosives beneath the Capitol.

President Abraham Lincoln.

Photograph, Anthony Berger, 1864. Library of Congress Prints and Photographs Division, LC-DIG-ppmsca-19305.

Meanwhile the Presid. elect was on his way to the Capital, where the Peace Convention was now assembled discussing measures that might lead to conciliation & Union;[9] the prospect was truly discouraging for the Seceded States were daily confirming their treasonous conduct by new acts—A Constitution had been formed and Mr. Jeff. Davis styled President—[10]His Inaugural appeared in the Northern press alongside of the speeches of Mr. Lincoln to the people on his way—

Most suddenly Mr. Lincoln appears in Wash. having avoided the assigned course of travel—he had been warned that his life would be endangered in Baltimore, and there is every reason to believe from the subsequent conduct of its mob that such should have been the case.

---

[9] In January, as a last attempt to avoid war, politicians explored options for a peace conference. On 19 January, Virginia invited delegates to attend a conference to start on 4 February. Although more than 100 delegates attended, none came from states of the Deep South, and the conference adjourned without any new proposals to resolve the crisis. Instead, it suggested an amendment to the Constitution that would extend the Missouri Compromise line and make other guarantees for the perpetuation of slavery in the United States. Potter, *The Impending Crisis*, 507, 545–47.

[10] In Montgomery, AL, the seceded states drafted a provisional constitution and selected Mississippian and former Secretary of War Jefferson Davis as provisional president. Davis was inaugurated on 18 February 1861.

Soon after the Peace Convention adjourned, with earnest conviction in many parts of the country that it had achieved peace & reunion

The Month of March was not barren of incident—though differing from had previously occurred—Mr Lincoln was inaugurated as peaceably as any of his predecessors,—but the realm was divided—I stood quietly on Penn. Avenue and watched the procession passing with all the customary parade.—The attention of the whole Country was now bent on Sumter—South Carolina required instant evacuation and the insolent demand was sustained by her confederates;—The North appeared undecided upon any particular course,—many seemed willing to let the possession of the Fort go by default, and Senator Douglas[11] even announced in his place that it could not be relieved and had not one month's provisions; even Charleston was quiescent under the same impression—but there was one honest & true heart who knew that the lawful authority of the U.S. should not be impugned with his consent that he as President would uphold it to the last—

As so came in the month of April 1861—At this time I had only seen Mr. Lincoln at a distance,–the throng that gathered about him for various purposes was impenetrable. On the 2[d] he came down to the Ordnance—just then I was not in the building and after looking around briefly he departed—Next evening however there was to be a wedding in the quarters of the Commandant[12] The President was invited but did not arrive until the ceremony was over; The spacious rooms were filled to their utmost—uniforms and rich dresses abounded—Mr Lincoln received marked attention and entered fully into the spirit of the evening—In the course of the evening I was introduced,—in the kindest manner he took my hand in both of his as if we had been friends for years—just meeting—and an easy off hand conversation ensued & continued until interrupted by the claims of others.

Beneath that calm and pleasant manner must have lain heavy thoughts,—for the measures to relieve Pickens & Sumter had just been decided on and the

[11] Stephen A. Douglas (D-IL).

[12] The marriage was of Navy Yard commandant Capt. Franklin Buchanan's daughter. Dahlgren noted in his diary that he talked with Lincoln for half an hour. Madeleine Vinton Dahlgren, *Memoir of John A. Dahlgren: Rear-Admiral United States Navy* (Boston: James R. Osgood and Company, 1882), 329.

orders had been given—[13]

A few days later the *Powhatan* put to sea—followed by some other steamers the object of these movements was only suspected by the Northern public—but the South was better informed and the usual supply of provisions from the Charleston market was at once cut off from Sumter—Virginia demanded to know of the President what he intended to do—and again attention was drawn to the furtive designs of the disunionists upon the Capital—leaders of daring & unscrupulous character such as Ben M^c^Cullough[14] were noticed about the precincts of the city entering & leaving at unusual hours

Wash^n.^ was again excited by the evident signs of approaching trouble the calls for Volunteers were responded to,— but no sympathy for the Fed. Gov^t^. was exhibited strongly—many of the Volunteers even refused to take the oath of allegiance to the U.S—Gen. Scott continued fully alive to the critical condition of things and all the approaches of the city were picketted—The Patent office, and Treasury were garrisoned by regulars as well as possible—their lower entrances barricaded

Still it was manifest to the least observant that the whole force which the Gov. could muster in Wash. served for little more than a police—not at all equal to an effective defence—

At last the storm broke—Sumter was summoned on the 11th—Anderson refused and on the next day So. Car. struck the blow which she & the South have since so bitterly repented—[15]

On the 14th the U.S. flag came down from its staff on Sumter—

The President hesitated not—the Proclamation that called out 75000 men drew the line at once between loyal and disloyal men—

13 Secessionist forces had seized federal property across the South and surrounded other installations. Federal garrisons remained in possession of Fort Sumter, SC, and Fort Pickens, FL. Until the end of March, when the situation of the garrisons became critical, the government had failed to force the issue; federal authorities feared that reinforcement or resupply might provoke war. At the start of April, expeditions to relieve both places were organized. Potter, *The Impending Crisis*, 575–76.

14 Ben McCullough, by turns a Texas Ranger, scout, Indian fighter, sheriff, and U.S. marshal, enjoyed a national reputation. After the secession of Texas, rumors quickly spread that McCullough aimed to launch a raid on Washington with Texas Rangers. While he ventured to Richmond, VA, briefly in April 1861, he spent most of the month in New Orleans, procuring small arms for Texas forces. Thomas W. Cutrer, *Ben McCullough and the Frontier Military Tradition* (Chapel Hill: University of North Carolina Press, 1993), 189–92.

15 Maj. Robert Anderson, commander, Fort Sumter, refused Confederate demands to surrender. On 12 April, Confederate forces opened fire on the fort. Without prospect of resupply or reinforcement, Anderson surrendered on 14 April.

Had Virginia remained true, there would have been little trouble or bloodshed in compelling the states that had seceded, to return—and yet the great result would never have been gained which now ensures tranquillity—slavery would have continued the reproach and the danger of the Republic—

The Act of Secession was passed in secret Session by Virginia Convention and though not made public, became known to the disloyal men of Maryland & the District[16]

The Capital & Gov. were now in imminent jeopardy—placed as they were in the midst of a disloyal and aggressive population—only separated by the Potomac from Virginia, while Maryland stood ready to bar the way from the North, whenever the moment was deemed opportune—The Mayor of Baltimore[17] enjoined the people to keep the peace, but his Proclamation said not a word of the Union—the troops in Wash. amounted to less than a thousand including Marines—Volunteers of the District were more numerous but the majority were probably not to be relied on in the event of a collision;—on the 18th about 500 Penn. Vols. had arrived—But next day when the Mass. 6th attempted to pass through Baltimore the true temper of that city was displayed—the mob attacked the regiment ferociously and was met by some well placed volleys which put an end to the fray until the travellers were able to pursue their journey but a Penn. regiment having no arms was driven back—So the Capital was thus isolated for the while from all help—and if Virginia and Maryland moved promptly what could save it to the Union?—[18]surely not the Thousand Regulars and 1300 Northern volunteers which now constituted the garrison—

The day previously a body of Virginia troops had seized the Arsenal at Harper's Ferry—and at this critical and gloomy period the safety of the Navy Yard seemed menaced by the resignation of its Commandant & Officers[19]

I was seated in my office much occupied in making dispositions of arms and ammunition suitable to the exigency when a confidential messenger from the Navy Department entered—with a message that the Department distrusted the

---

[16] The Virginia Convention went into secret session on 16 April 1861 and the next day voted to secede. Virginia voters would later approve the ordinance in May.

[17] George William Brown.

[18] A mob in Baltimore, of Southern sympathies, attacked the 6th Massachusetts Infantry Regiment and attempted to block the passage of other regiments heading to Washington.

[19] Capt. Franklin Buchanan, commandant of the Washington Navy Yard, resigned following the attack on Fort Sumter. Virginia troops occupied the armory at Harper's Ferry on 18 April 1861.

state of affairs in the Yard and directed me to take the command—[20] I replied that the Dep might fully rely on me, and at once sallied out to view things and take proper measures—not long so employed when a messenger came to say that the Commandant wished to see me—for I had considered it my duty to take command and to exercise it without concerning myself about the authority of any one else—On reaching the Comdts. office he said that he was about to resign and wished to turn over the command to me—very few words passed and I once more resumed operations for defence[21]

The Government held Washington by a most precarious tenure—With small exception the population could not be expected to sympathise with the North.—and illy suppressed open manifestation—the troops that could be relied on to fight for the U.S. did not exceed 2000 to 2500 men half of which were entirely inexperienced—the prize was great for if the South were to occupy Wash^{n} it would offer to foreign nations the semblance of the legitimate Gov^{t}.—and might be sure of recognition by France & England at least—the last restraint on Maryland would be removed and she would be added to the active rebellion—The Richmond press was urgent for instant measures—the loyal press even announced that there was "imminent danger that the Fed. metropolis might be wrested from the Gov"—and that such was "a leading feature in the plans of the revolutionists"

All communication with the North by land was severed—as the R. road bridges above Baltim. were broken and that city was rampant—the river alone offered a chance for passage of friends—Whatever force Virginia could raise might be precipitated on the city immediately—The Potomac only lay between—

A glance at a map of the locality will show that the Navy Yard lies on the extreme left of and rather more than a mile from the city as it faces to the South—it lies immediately along the Anacostia, a branch of the Potomac,—which separates it from the country opposite,—known as the Eastern shore of Maryland—a region thoroughly imbued with the slavery and disunion proclivities of the South, and not better disposed probably even to the present time—the connection between the two sides of the river was established by a bridge immediately above the Navy Yard,—four or five hundred resolute men passing over suddenly could not fail to cut off and obtain possession of the Yard—which was assailable

[20] In his diary, Dahlgren identified the messenger as one of Gideon Welles's sons, who carried word that "his father desired me to take command, as there was something wrong going on in the Yard." Dahlgren, *Memoirs of John A. Dahlgren*, 330–31.

[21] Before Buchanan resigned, he ordered Dahlgren to "superintend the defense of the yard when necessary." ORN 4: 418.

"U.S. Gun Boat *Pawnee*." Drawing on paper; Alfred R. Waud, c. 1861.

Morgan collection of Civil War drawings, Library of Congress, Prints and Photographs Division, LC-DIG-ppmsca-20335.

on every side—On the North and it was enclosed by a brick wall of no great height—which could be scaled easily or forced at the gates;— the south side was washed by the river and in the West was an old and infirm wooden fence—just where all the Ordnance stores—of artillery, rifles and Powder were to be found—

The Marine barracks about 600 yards from the Northern wall would have served as a strong support in case of attack, but it had been stripped of its garrison of Marines from the 19th to the 24th of April, who had been sent in the *Pawnee* to assist in the destruction of the Norfolk Navy Yard—[22]

During this critical period the defence of the Washington Yard depended upon some 50 Seamen in the Ordn Dep. and about 40 Marines—with such aid as could be had from two small War Steamers in the stream, whose crews did not probably exceed 150 men.[23] The small detachment of District volunteers would rather have embarrassed the defence—

To obtain possession of the Yard was to open an easy way to the City on the

[22] Commo. Hiram Paulding embarked 100 Marines on *Pawnee*, and steamed for Norfolk, VA, to prevent the supplies and vessels at the navy yard there from falling into enemy hands. See ORN 4: 284–85, 289–91.

[23] *Anacostia*, a packet under the command of Lt. Thomas Scott Fillebrown; and *Pocahontas*, under the command of Cmdr. John P. Gillis. ORN 4: 410–11 and 419.

East—and at the same time would have been attended with the loss of ordnance Stores indispensable for the supply of the whole U.S Navy, which would also have been invaluable to the attack,—for there was on hand a number of new Brass Howitzers and breech-loadg rifles with powder and every kind of Ammunition—

While the various steamboats & other craft at the wharf would have instantly furnished the means of holding the river & all the water communications to the city—

Whilst this post not so important to the defence of the City,—I received no support therefrom—not even to keep open the communication of about a mile through an open country—

It is difficult to understand why the revolt omitted to strike a prompt blow at the National capital—Many times afterward it seemed in great peril, but in reality never so much as in these days—

The sudden abandonment of their duty by <u>all</u> the officers of the Yard (for I belonged to the Ordnance) at the most critical portion of this period, seemed to offer a desirable opportunity—

It was just at this eventful crisis that the command was devolved on me—by those who hardly knew me by sight[24]—Yet I can say truly that at this most gloomy period not a misgiving crossed my mind but that the defence would be made good to the last—whether successful or not

I lost no time in looking to the first important points—Two Howitzers were sent to the bridge and planted so as to rake it with Canister—manned by seamen who I knew perfectly, could & would fire canister at the rate of seven to 10 shots in a minute—they were supported by a small detachment of riflemen—pickets were placed along the line of wall—Boat Howitzers at the weak points—The two small War steamers in the stream could bring their guns to bear upon the bridge, or upon the approaches to the Yard by the Western side—

A strong force of mechanics was thrown upon the river steamers of the Mail line which had been seized,[25] so as to equip them to assist in keeping command of the Potomac, now our only communication unobstructed—they were too weak as they were to receive a single cannon—so the decks were well shored and a 32 pdr placed on board—this was kept going all day and by night too—Coal, water & provisions were hurried on board, and before night of the day I

[24] Commandant Franklin Buchanan resigned on 22 April 1861.

[25] The Army had seized the steamers *Baltimore, Mount Vernon, Philadelphia*, and *Powhatan* on 21 April 1861, at the direction of President Lincoln. They soon turned them over to the Navy, and Dahlgren had "been directed to have them equipped for war service forthwith." ORN 4: 416–17.

"U.S. Steamer *Mt Vernon* (Washington & Fortress Monroe line)." Drawing on paper; Alfred R. Waud, 1861.

Morgan collection of Civil War drawings, Library of Congress, Prints and Photographs Division, LC-DIG-ppmsca-20339.

took command, one of these vessels (the *Mt Vernon*) was ready for service and at midnight I sent her down the river to capture suspicious craft[,][26] to observe the movements of the disunionists and to give pilots to any vessels that might be coming with troops from the North to the relief of the Capital—Having no officers to aid me, I put her in command of an old Boatswain—Wilmuth—one of those samples of seamen whom we in the Navy like to look upon—Time had whitened his locks, but had not bleached his ruddy visage nor abated his vigor—nor his allegiance to the Flag— This veteran probably fired the first hostile shot at rebeldom in this quarter[27]

Night came, and the mechanics passed out of the yard as usual to their homes, but the work on the steamers continued, as well as the use of precautions to prevent surprise, and it was near midnight when I laid down on a sofa in my office to snatch a little sleep—

The next day brought no change or improvement of the condition of the Yard—I was constantly moving around observing all that passed and urging the

---

[26] Secretary of the Navy Gideon Welles had given instructions to Dahlgren on the use of *Mount Vernon* on 22 April 1861. ORN 4: 419.

[27] Boatswain George Willmuth. *Mount Vernon* fired muskets and a shell at a boat that had set the lightship at Cedar Point, MD, on fire. Willmuth's complete report can be found in ORN 4: 425–26.

Men of the 71st New York form a hollow square at the Washington Navy Yard in 1861. *James Guy* is moored on the right, *Powhatan* is at left.

Photograph c. 1861, printed c. 1880. Library of Congress, Prints and Photographs Division, LC-DIG-ppmsca-34786.

equipment of the remaining Mail steamers—The City was in confusion & excitement—reports that the rebels were attempting to obstruct the Potomac—The resignation of many officers was made known, among them Gen. Johnson, Col. Robt Lee &c—[28]some troops were known to have arrived at Annapolis, but it was not sure that they would reach here without opposition—for we had no communication with the North in any way—To day the Gov. took possession of the Railroad at this place—

The critical condition was gradually improved but it cannot be said to any material extent until the last day of the week—

On Thursday the 25th the communication with the North by land was effectively opened by the arrival of the 7th N. York at Washington and the occupation of the Railroad from Annapolis by Gen. Butler with Mass. and other troops—On Saturday. the 27th the 71st New. York reached the Navy Yard and Col. Vosburgh reported his regiment to me to assist in the defence of the Yard—[29]

28 Brig. Gen. Joseph E. Johnston, Quartermaster General at the time of his resignation, and Col. Robert E. Lee, who held command of the 1st Cav.

29 Col. Abram S. Vosburgh and the 71st New York State Militia arrived in Washington and were posted at the Washington Navy Yard on 27 April 1861. [Augustus Theodore Francis], *History of the 71st Regiment, N.G., N.Y.* (New York: The Veterans Association, 71st Regiment, N.G.N.Y., 1919), 124–25.

Previously I had received slight temporary aid in other ways—one of them was a Reading Co. of Volunteers commanded by Capt McKnight—composed of as fine material as I ever saw[30]

One night a citizen Company spent with me—made up of gentlemen then visiting Wash—and brought together by that then zealous patriot Gen. Lane and Col. Cassius Clay—they had buckled and belted bayonet and cartridge box over the ordinary garb of the citizen[31]—part of them I posted at the bridge and the remainder along the weaker defences of the Yard—where they did watch and ward until the next day relieved them—

Meanwhile the Capitol and all the Public buildings were occupied by the troops newly arrived—which rendered them strongholds—barricaded with barrels of Cement and with other material that was convenient—while the Senate Chamber and the Represen. Hall and the offices were crowded with armed men—who ate & slept there and made the outer courts ring with their heavy muskets—

During this anxious period I entered not my regular quarters but slept and ate in the office near the Wharf, or on board of a steamer alongside, just where the work of the closing day found me—The activity was incessant in every Department—between defence, against surprise and in preparation for Naval supplies of all kinds—

Meanwhile Maryland continued to confirm the disunion position first taken

On Sunday I was out of the Yard for the first time since the trouble began, and only for a short time to see the President—Deeply concerned in passing events, he was as composed as a Veteran and nothing daunted, was declaring his position as each emergency arose—just now appeared his Proclam.— blockading

[30] Capt. James McKnight commanded the Ringgold Artillery, a Pennsylvania militia company from Reading. The Ringgold Artillery and other Pennsylvania militia units arrived quickly in Washington after the Civil War began. John David Hoptak, "The Union's First Defenders," *Pennsylvania Heritage* Vol. 39 No. 3 (Summer 2013), 5–15.

[31] James Henry Lane had been elected senator from Kansas in April 1861, but had not yet been seated. Both Lane and Kentucky politician Cassius M. Clay were committed anti-slavery advocates and had previous military experience; Lane had led Free-Soil militia in "Bleeding Kansas" during the 1850s, while Clay had fought in the Mexican-American War. Both men raised volunteer companies to defend Washington from secessionists. Assistant Adjutant General Thomas Talbot had ordered Clay and Lane to report to the Navy Yard on 24 April 1861, instructing them: "you will report to the commandant of the Navy Yard . . . on each succeeding night for the periods that your respective commands may have been enrolled." Cassius M. Clay, *Cassius Marcellus Clay: Memoirs, Writings, and Speeches*, Vol. 1 (Cincinnati: J. Fletcher Brennan & Co., 1886), 262.

the coasts of Virginia & N.C.—[32]I found him in the Cabinet-Room and had a brief conversation with him alone—

The closing of U.S troops about Baltimore, enabled the Gov. to restore the communication by Railroad through the city by the 10th of May—And so the Capital was finally re-connected with its true Base, the North and the troops which had now gathered sufficed to make it sure—

The cause of the Union had now passed its hour of peril and the power of the loyal States could be put forth to crush the Rebellion—

The Wash. press[33] stated that the plan of the Insurgents had been to enter Wash. between the 18th and 21st of April before day break but some failure to adjust the parts of their scheme postponed it until too late—

My service on this occasion I count as the best which I ever rendered to the country—

Ulric Dahlgren, son of John A. Dahlgren, in the uniform of an Army captain.

Glass negative, c. 1862. Brady Photograph Collection, National Archives, B-6209.

On the 6th of May I had the pleasure of a visit from Major Anderson—

[32] Lincoln ordered the blockade of ports in Alabama, Florida, Georgia, Louisiana, Mississippi, South Carolina, and Texas on 19 April 1861. After the secession of Virginia and North Carolina he ordered that "an efficient blockade of the ports of those States will therefore also be established." ORN 4: 340.

[33] JAD: "Star. May 6th." The article claimed that "the scheme of the oligarchy was to have attacked this city some time between daybreak of the 18th and daybreak of the 21st April ultimo . . . The conspirators had no idea that the Government would prove more prompt and efficient in their measures of defense, than they in theirs of attack." The newspaper mentioned Governor John Letcher of Virginia as a conspirator, as well as John Bell of Tennessee, the former candidates for president of the Constitutional Union Party in the 1860 election. *Evening Star* (Washington, DC), 6 May 1861, 2.

fresh from Sumter—and my son Ulric also came down from his law studies at Philad.—anxious to do such duty to his country as a lad could offer

The Anacostia & the Potomac are now alive with movement—large steamers arriving & landing troops, cannon and stores of all kinds at the Arsenal and Navy Yard—every where is heard & seen the signs of War—The Rebel flag too can be perceived floating over Alexandria—we shall pull it down soon—[34]

On the 9th of May the President came down to a Concert given by the 71st N.Y. who still formed part of the garrison of the Yard—In some way or another quite a number of ladies & gentlemen collected too and well filled the lower floor of the Navy Store which was made to serve the purpose temporarily—The singers were all of the Regiment and did the thing in good style—Mr Lincoln enjoyed it very much and afterwards asked to see some practice from the battery with the XIin gun—I could offer him no hospitality for my quarters were still in the Office—

A few days afterwards the President came down in his usual off hand way and sat some while in the office conversing with me on various matters, among other things he expressed anxiety lest the insurgents should raise batteries to obstruct the Potomac[35]—So next day I went down early in a steamer and examined some of the points where this might be likely to occur—A few days [later] Capt. Ward arrived with two little armed Steamers and kept an eye along the river banks—[36]

On the 24th the move on Alexandria took place as previously determined:—The night before I was to send down steamboats to Giesborough Point for the Zouave Regiment,[37] which was to land at the Alex. wharves at the same time that a column passing over the Long Bridge should enter the upper part of the city

To prevent mishaps as far as possible in the embarcation,—for all were new to the business, I went down myself to supervise the operation—It was midnight

---

34 Possibly the secession banner flown from the Marshall House, a hotel in Alexandria. The banner could be seen from the vicinity of the Navy Yard. "*With the 11th New York Fire Zouaves in Camp, Battle, and Prison: The Narrative of Private Arthur O'Neil Alcock*" in The New York Atlas and Leader, ed. Brian C. Pohanka and Patrick A. Schroeder (Lynchburg, VA: Schroeder Publications, 2011), 94.

35 This visit took place on 18 May. Dahlgren, *Memoir of John A. Dahlgren*, 333.

36 Cmdr. James H. Ward left the New York Navy Yard on 17 May with *Thomas Freeborn* and an unidentified small propeller-driven ship and arrived at the Washington Navy Yard on 20 May. ORN 4: 467, 471.

37 The 11th NY Inf. Regt. The regiment wore the distinctive outfit of the Zouaves, who were French North African light infantry auxiliaries. They wore fezzes, bright red pantaloons, and special jackets. Col. Elmer Ellsworth had popularized the style in America before the Civil War, leading a drill team that demonstrated the unique light infantry drill of the Zouaves.

when the steamboats got to the Point—Ellsworth was afoot and in the act of forming one of the companies, the rest of his regiment was soon aroused—[38] but it took some time to get the men aboard—it was well that we had a bright moon—I invited Ellsworth into my own boat, the *Guy*, which carried no troops—[39]the steamers now moved down the river, and I looked towards the Long Bridge for some sign of the column that was to cross—but it was too dark—Col. Ellsworth & myself conversed quietly about the business in hand and when near the wharf I put him in one of the steamboats with his men at his own request—I caused the vessels to move no faster than would just bring us to the wharf by break of day—the Howitzers of my own steamboat were trained so as to sweep with Canister, if any sign of resistance appeared,—presently we were close to,—a few musket shots were fired from the rebel sentries,—the steamers ran alongside—the Zouaves jumped ashore and entered the narrow alleys—there was no defence I waited to be sure—and finding that our men were in possession, I went on board the *Pawnee* at anchor off the town and laid down on a sofa to catch a few moments of sleep—for I had been up nearly all night—It seemed as if I was hardly asleep when a quarter Master awakened me with word that Ellsworth was killed—[40]I got ashore quickly and hurrying up into the town, met a detail of Zouaves carrying the body of their Colonel to the wharf—I directed them to my own steamer, and returned to the Navy Yard—It seemed strange, though we had been together & conversed—I had never seen his face—it was too dark during the night and now he had been sewed up in a coarse blanket[41]

The enterprise had been entirely successful—the U.S. troops had occupied Alexandria and the contiguous country without opposition—some 500 or 600 rebs in the town escaped but a troop of Fairfax Cavalry was captured and sent to

38 For an account of the embarkation and travel to Alexandria, see Pohanka and Schroeder, "*With the 11th New York*," 92–96, 98.

39 Steamer *James Guy*, commanded by Acting Master David C. Woods. *Pocahontas* had picked it up on Machadoc Creek, VA suspecting the loyalty of its owner. ORN 4: 472, 475, 477.

40 Ellsworth had entered the Marshall House, intent on removing the secession banner seen from the camp of the 11th NY Inf.. As he made his way down the stairs after tearing the banner down, James Jackson, the proprietor of the hotel shot and killed him with a shot to the heart. In turn, one of Ellsworth's men killed Jackson. Pohanka and Schroeder, "*With the 11th New York*," 99.

41 Arthur O'Neil Alcock, a newspaper correspondent, gave an account of the removal of Ellsworth's body from Alexandria, and discussed the activities of a shore party from *Pawnee*. Ibid., 95-96, 99.

"Action between the US vessels *Pawnee* and *Freeborn* and the rebel batteries at Acquæ Creek." The captions written by Waud along the top of the image, from left to right, "gun boat *Freeborn*," "rebel batteries," "R.R. depot and Long dock on fire," "rebel batteries," and "US. Sloop *Pawnee*." Alfred R. Waud, 1861.

Morgan collection of Civil War drawings, Library of Congress, Prints and Photographs Division, LC-DIG-ppmsca-21146.

the Navy Yard—[42]

Without delay the engineers were at work intrenching the line of Heights that encircle Wash: on the S.W. and the numerous regiments that had been collecting in Washington pour over Long Bridge and extended themselves along the new position—Thus the National Capital was effectively assured against the any effort that could be made to take it—

In the afternoon the President drove to the Yard—He had known Ellsworth and his kindly nature was shocked and grieved at the suddenness and manner of his death—After some conversation with me he asked, if it be proper to have the funeral service at the White House—I advised him that it would be proper to consult his feelings solely—he concluded to do so—and the necessary orders

[42] Union forces captured 38 Confederates of the cavalry troop under the command of Capt. M. Dulany Ball. Ibid., 96. Dahlgren's report on the expedition is found at ORN 4: 477.

were given—Next day the body was transferred to the White House and the fitting rites were performed

On the 1st of June the oath of allegiance to the Gen[eral]. Gov[ernment]. was tendered to the workmen of the Navy Yard in my presence—out of 700 or 800 only three refused—they were expelled immediately—The presence of 100,000 Union bayonets had had the effect of settling opinion the right way—

About this time the rebs. began to manifest more decided intentions towards the river—and batteries were observable at Acquia probably to protect the terminus of the Rail Road and its buildings—this attracted our cruisers under Captain Ward and straightway he went at them with his little vessels and their metal was however too light to make much impression, but it showed Ward's good will and he gave them little rest—[43]

In the first week of June, I was authorised to release the Virginia troop of Cavalry, taken prisoners when we seized Alexandria—during their captivity every care had been taken to make it as light as possible,—they were 35 in number and were well accommodated in the *Powhatan*, one of the Mail steamers that used to run between Washington and Acquia—the thousands of passengers that have travelled in this Boat knew the ample extent of her two Cabins, Upper & Lower—The Officers had State rooms and some of the others—The Guard was taken from the 71st—they lived and sat down to the same table as the Virginians—letters went and came without restraint—When Capt. Ball's mother & wife came to my office and asked to see him,—I sent on board the *Powhatan*, invited him ashore, and assigned him, a room opposite my own where he could spend as much of the day as he chose with his family—I gave orders to admit no one on board whom the prisoners did not wish to see—for artists and reporters were as usual invading every corner—in fact nothing was omitted to soften the rigors of captivity—and finally in my many opportunities with the President I lost no one to urge their release—these things are not recapitulated with a view to any credit therefor, but as an instance of the feeling that prevailed towards men whose hands were not then red with the dearest blood of the land—[44]

On the 27th we lost that gallant officer Ward—his efforts to keep the river

43 Cmdr. James Ward's reports on his attacks on the Confederate batteries at Aquia Creek, VA, are in ORN 4: 490–91 and 491–92.

44 Dahlgren may have been at pains to explain that he treated the prisoners well because M. Dulany Ball publicized a statement after his release alleging poor treatment. Among other things, he claimed that "while prisoner we were exposed to constant insults . . . we were assured the Federal forces were in possession of our homes and our families had been driven out; we could hear nothing from our friends." OR Series 2, Vol. 3:684–85.

"Capt Wards pet 32 pdr which he took aboard the *Freeborn*—& met his death close to it." Also noted below Ward: "all caps are felt hats Navy Yard N.Y." The sketch at bottom is labelled: "carrying sails aboard Navy Yard." Drawing on paper, Alfred R. Waud, 1861.

Morgan collection of Civil War drawings, Library of Congress, Prints and Photographs Division, LC-DIG-ppmsca-21514.

clear and to cut off communications between its shores had been unceasing he seemed ubiquitous with two or three little steamers—his best gun a 32pdr:—most troublesome menaced Matthias Point—a bluff, heavily wooded tongue of land that projected out in the river forming a turn in the channel—& compelling it to wind at short range around its extreme—batteries here would close navigation—so all attention was given to that—Ward wished to anticipate any movement of the rebs. to this effect,—he planned an attack,—asked for military aid—did not get it—made the landing himself—came in contact with an overwhelming force, ten to his one to his own before which his little party wilted away—Ward was close by with his little gunboat—and opened fire from her only 32pdr—to cover his men—the Captain of the gun was shot & fell—Ward stepped into his place, and just as he stooped to aim the gun, a ball pierced his body,—he fell, was carried aft—and lived but an hour—thus this country lost one whose courage, zeal and ability could illy be spared—and one of whom too little has been said—The remains of the heroic officer were brought to the Yard, and received from me all the honors in my power—[45]

And now the City and the camps that whitened every surrounding hill were alive to the coming trial,—the cry was on to Richmond,—and the public would not be satisfied with aught else—

The press publishes a list of every regiment that has reached Wash$^{n.}$—amounting to some 56,000 men by the 1st July—so that the enemy need not trouble himself to spy out our real condition

At last came the 21st July—it was well known then that the Army, perhaps 50,000 strong had advanced—and would soon come to blows—

It was a fine quiet Sunday, and as the 71st had left the Yard, it was perfectly quiet—About 6^{OC} in the evening the President drove down for the ride, and in the course of conversation said that the battle had begun—he had telegrams from the field and all was going well He had not left the Yard half an hour when I had a telegram from Gen. Mansfield asking me to send a vessel with dispatch to Alexandria to cover the approaches—this looked badly—[46]as if our army was being forced back—I had nothing but the *Perry*, just arrived and she was hurried down;[47] gradually the worst of the tidings arrived—and before daylight some of the 71st got to the Navy Yard—

The next day was a "black Monday" truly—the Army had lost no time in falling back on the lines,—the city was filled with fugitive soldiers—whose tales were well calculated to alarm the citizens—the rain fell in torrents,—and the hopes of the Republic looked gloomy enough—[48]

It was about 10^{OC} when the 71st returned to the Yard—that is what was left of it in an organised form—perhaps not the force of two companies,—seemingly worn out with hunger and fatigue—food was soon provided for them and sleep followed—the officers were gathered into my own quarters to a hasty lunch and

---

45 Cmdr. Ward, of *Thomas Freeborn*, fell in action against Confederate forces at Mathias Point, VA. A Navy landing party had gone ashore there and soon faced an overwhelming Confederate response. Ward brought *Thomas Freeborn* in close ashore to cover the withdrawal from the beach. Cmdr. Stephen C. Rowan, in his after-action report, wrote that Ward had been "shot in the abdomen while in the act of sighting his bow gun." F. M. Gunnell, a Navy surgeon, remarked that the wound had been "almost immediately fatal." ORN 4: 537, 538, 540.

46 Brig. Gen. Joseph K. F. Mansfield's telegram is in OR 2: 751.

47 *Perry* and a steam tug left the Washington Navy Yard for Alexandria, VA, on 21 July 1861. ORN 4: 582.

48 On 21 July 1861, Union forces under Brig. Gen. Irvin McDowell had been defeated by Confederate forces under Gens. P. G. T. Beauregard and Joseph E. Johnston at the Battle of Manassas. The Union troops left the field in some disorder, hurrying back into the defenses of Washington.

there I listened with deep interest to the various accounts of what passed—In the course of the day numbers of the regiment dropped in by parties large & small or even in pairs—it was a fine regiment and must have endured much in the days work—

The disorganization that prevailed was complete—one who should know, describes a woful ignorance of the first elements of military life,—on some of the main roads to the city there were no troops at all—the camps were located without regard to defence,—the roads not picketed,—in no quarters would the defence have been even respectable against vigorous attack—"There was nothing to prevent the enemy shelling the city from heights within easy range, which could be occupied by a hostile column almost without resistance,—the streets of Wash. were crowded with straggling officers and men &c"[49]

In the sad scene of disorder and helplessness the first resort was to the soldier who had so vigorously overborne the rebel cause in Western Virginia and the telegraph summoned M^c^Clellan to Washington on the day after the battle[50]

The Navy was called on to contribute its assistance—and I sent down three IX^in^ ship cannon and five Howitzers, with a body of trained seamen and some Marines—in short time they arrived in Steamers at Alexandria—and the heavy guns drawn by Oxen, the Howitzers by hand were marching for the lines—on the contiguous range of hills—this ends abruptly about a mile from the town, leaving a flat open country by which an enemy could turn the whole of our fortified line,—the Navy Battery was planted just at this point—so as to check such a flank move—[51]I had given the command to Captain Foxhall Parker, a most excellent officer—who quickly completed the arrangements for the new position, and put his command in such effective order as to render his post impregnable—On this occasion my gallant boy Ulric Dahlgren only 19 years old made his first essay as an Aid to Capt. Parker—[52]

[49] This information was drawn from Maj. Gen. George B. McClellan's report on conditions in Washington when he took command. Dahlgren's dash in the quotation elides the following phrase: "Many soldiers had deserted, and." OR 5: 11.

[50] McClellan led Union forces to victory in the Rich Mountain Campaign in West Virginia; after McDowell's defeat at Bull Run, Lincoln placed McClellan in command of the newly-created Army of the Potomac.

[51] The naval force at Fort Ellsworth consisted of a battery of three IX-inch guns, five howitzers, 110 seamen, and 50 Marines, all under the command of Lt. Foxhall Parker. ORN 4: 589. Parker's report on the expedition can be found in [John A.] Dahlgren, *Memoir of Ulric Dahlgren* (Philadelphia: J. B. Lippincott & Co., 1872), 44–47.

[52] Ulric Dahlgren arrived in Washington on 1 July 1861. When Parker was sent to Fort Ellsworth, Ulric volunteered to accompany him as an aide. Ibid., 40.

Gideon Welles, Lincoln's Secretary of the Navy.

Glass negative, c. 1860. Brady-Handy Photograph Collection, Library of Congress, Prints and Photographs Division, LC-DIG-cwpbh-01102.

In about a couple of weeks after the battle of Bull Run confidence and order were restored, and the Gov. began to collect an Army that would be equal to the task before it—

Early in August, Congress manifested its sense of my service, by a special act enabling me to hold command of the Wash. Navy Yard,—for by law no one below the rank of Captain could do so and I was only a Commander—[53]

And a day or two later the Navy Depart. offered me the Bureau of Ordnance, but I preferred the Yard in every way for Washn. had again become the centre of great operations,—and the importance conferred on the Yard, made it equal to any naval trust that could be given so I declined—[54]

The rebels perceiving the probable inability of our Army to move for some time—covered the country up to our very lines and began to look seriously to obstructing the river communications—now very important for the transportation of much of the vast material required by an army of nearly two

[53] House Resolution 78, 37th Congress, 1st Session, amended the 1804 authorization for a naval peace establishment "so that the President shall be authorized to select the superintendent of the navy yard at Washington from captains or commanders of the navy of the United States." As Dahlgren indicated here, previously the language had limited selection to captains. It passed on 2 August. Robert J. Schneller Jr., *A Quest for Glory: A Biography of Rear Admiral John A. Dahlgren* (Annapolis, MD: Naval Institute Press, 1996), 187.

[54] This offer came from Welles on 5 August. Ibid.

hundred thousand—

There were indications also of a purpose to cross a rebel force into the Eastern shore, known to be disaffected and thus menace Washington from another quarter—

By the middle of September the rebels had occupied ground close in our front and the flag of Rebeldom was plainly visible from the ship-house of the Navy Yard—this brought out skirmishers from both sides and some sharp work ensued—Ulric Dahlgren tired of the regular & undisturbed life of the post,—circulated among some friends in the Camp and was daily in the outer skirmish line about Munson's Hill, with his rifle.—where his good aim and activity exposed others as well as himself[55]

Among our friends from abroad we have the Prince de Joinville & his nephew[56]—the large number of officers and distinguished civilians collected in the city give occasion to continued reunions in the evening and to dinners—

The conduct & discipline of the Navy at our battery in the lines has been so satisfactory that Gen. McClellan desired to hand over Fort Ellsworth to Naval occupation—So I was directed to take charge of it and sent down 600 sailors under the command of that truly gallant officer Lieut Wainwright—[57]

When October came the army was in condition to spread out and occupy more ground—the rebs. made no serious opposition and drew in their outposts toward Manassas—But at the same time came certain evidences that their batteries were going up on the river bank—those so long feared batteries

The necessities of this central position have gathered a number of Steamers at & off the Yard—some of the them altered from merchant vessels which work has much occupied my attention—for it is no small matter to convert such to war purposes—

We know too that the *Merrimac* has been raised and is being rapidly converted by the rebs. into an Ironclad—before me is a sketch of what report makes her,

---

[55] The flag visible from the Navy Yard was on Munson's Hill. On 5 September 1861, Ulric wrote that "I was in two skirmishes near Munson's Hill, in which we lost several killed and wounded, and they lost some also. It is regular Indian-fighting that we do every day near here, and I have a Maynard rifle, with which *I send a telegram* south occasionally." Dahlgren, *Memoir of Ulric Dahlgren*, 49–50.

[56] François, Prince de Joinville, son of King Louis Philippe of France. He served in the French navy and left France for England during the turmoil of the Revolution of 1848. Prince de Joinville, *Memoirs (Vieux Souvenirs) of the Prince de Joinville*, trans. Lady Mary Loyd (London: William Heinemann, 1895).

[57] A contingent of 400 additional men left the Washington Navy Yard for Fort Ellsworth on 28 August 1861. Lt. Richard Wainwright later took command. ORN 4: 642.

Rear Admiral Andrew H. Foote.

Glass negative, c. 1863. Brady Photograph Collection, National Archives, B-3859.

by a Navy officer of high rank—and now it seems to have been correct enough for our guidance.—We are just talking about iron-clads—but nothing done.[58]

Foote is at work out West—I have a letter from him—in which after speaking of movements expected he says "I expect of course to be shot by a Kentucky rifleman but I mean to die game as there must be a Providence in all these things"—he was hit but by something bigger than a rifle ball—[59]

By the middle of October the batteries showed their teeth—Rumor after rumor pointed to their existence and naturally much anxiety was felt on the subject for the navigation of the river would be seriously troubled

The *Pocahontas* & *Seminole* were to go down the river, and Drayton who commanded the former, being my friend from boyhood was staying with me—the breakfast was very early for his convenience in leaving—when over I accompanied him to the door—we laughed about the batteries—and the probability of their opening—he felt sure that they were ready, but he had no orders to disturb them by firing first—I replied laughing "Well I'll give you orders"—Drayton in great

[58] The Confederates raised *Merrimack* and converted her into the ironclad CSS *Virginia*.

[59] On 30 August 1861, Gideon Welles assigned Capt. Andrew Foote to command the naval forces on the western rivers, who set about creating a flotilla upon his arrival. Foote died from disease during the war. Spencer C. Tucker, *Andrew Foote: Civil War Admiral on Western Waters* (Annapolis, MD: Naval Institute Press, 2000), 114–21.

glee said—"Well I'll do it"[60]

The two vessels steamed down, *Pocahontas* ahead—presently they came opposite the suspect point—all was quiet, not a head visible—only a long row of trees—Drayton cast loose his heavy Pivot gun and deliberately put in one shell after another, while in range—Instantly men were seen—flying axes—down fell the trees, and the batteries appeared—blazing away finely,—but the *Pocahontas* having passed, the rebs aimed at the *Seminole*—hitting her several times—The *Pawnee* being about to follow filled with Marines, when Capt. Craven arrived from below with the news,—the men were transferred to light steamboats which I sent down after dark and passed safely—[61]

Percival Drayton later in the war, wearing the uniform of a captain. At Charleston, Drayton commanded *Pawnee* and *Passaic*. Glass negative, c. 1864.

Brady-Handy Photograph Collection, Library of Congress, Prints and Photographs Division, LC-DIG-cwpbh-03078.

A week later came the misadventure of Edward's Ferry—Gen. M^c^Clellan with a friend was taking a quiet dinner with me in my quarters at the Navy Yard and the evening was sliding away pleasantly in easy chat about matters, when the Yard telegraph conveyed a message from Col. Stone saying he had crossed a body of troops at Edwards Ferry: M^c^Clellan replied by the same way, and soon after concluded to return to his Headquarters—he had left but a short time when came another dispatch by Telegraph

[60] Gideon Welles, on 5 October, informed Dahlgren that Cmdr. Percival Drayton would receive command of *Pocahontas*; Drayton formally assumed command on 9 October. ORN 4: 703, 767.

[61] Cmdr. Thomas T. Craven commanded the Potomac Flotilla. Craven's report of this action, as well as that of Cmdr. John P. Gillis of *Seminole*, is found in ORN 4: 718–21. Dahlgren's instructions for *Pawnee* and the Marines are also found in ORN 4: 721–23.

"Steam sloop *Pensacola* brought to Washington under canvas from Pensacola, some time 1861." Drawing on paper; Alfred R. Waud, 1861.

Morgan collection of Civil War drawings, Library of Congress, Prints and Photographs Division, LC-DIG-ppmsca-20187.

["]Edward Ferry Oct. 21
Maj. Gen. McClellan

Col. Baker has been killed at the head of his Brigade. I go to the right at once—C.P. Stone

Brig. Gen["]

The public were as much distressed with this small affair as if it had been much greater,[62]— but was soon diverted to the interruption of the river, against which they clamored loudly—I offered to establish counter batteries on the Md. side,—but the military opinion properly considered these batteries a part of the reb. position and preferred to have them fall with it—direct attack could end in nothing of consequence—A strong Division was located opposite to prevent any

[62] On 21 October 1861, a small Union force suffered a defeat at Ball's Bluff, on the Potomac River in Loudoun County, VA. Col. Edward Baker, a sitting senator and friend of Abraham Lincoln, was killed during the fighting. Many blamed Brig. Gen. Charles P. Stone for the fiasco. Dissatisfaction with the progress of the Union's military endeavors, including the battles of First Manassas and Ball's Bluff, led Congress to establish the Joint Committee on the Conduct of the War, in an effort to exercise oversight of the war effort. Gary W. Gallgher, JCCW index vol., "Introduction," vi-vii.

connection with the rebs—

The Prince de Joinville often rides to the yard and seems entirely engrossed with our affairs—

By the middle of Novem the engine of the *Pensacola* was in condition for use and the President came down with several of the Cabinet and took a trip down the river

Foote began to be ready to move in the West and wanted seamen—no alternative but to withdraw the seamen from Fort Ellsworth and send them,—which was done—they were a fine body of men and served him well—

Just now the course of our affairs was disturbed by the seizure of Slidell & Mason creating much feeling—[63]the Diplomats all think against us, and show more feeling than good will—in the evening I dined with the Prince de J— he is a good friend and thinks England will not let us off easily—Many distinguished persons continue to visit the Yard—and scarcely a day passes but that I meet with our principal men, discussing our affairs, so that the company at Wash. never has been of like interest—The President everywhere—and always the same kind sagacious gentleman—I had occasion to observe in more than one instance how the Mason affair weighed on his spirits—

Our Christmas was not merry,—there was too much at stake—

A day or two afterward—the President came down, and proposed a trip down the river—no one was with him, so we went to the *Pensacola* and steamed as far as Craney I. then back—The President talked as much upon many subjects but forbore from the British trouble,—when we landed, he said "well there has been a pleasant day"—"such a relief from politicians—"[64]

Next day the whole matter was out—á soirée at the Dutch Ministry was fully attended except that our Sec. of State[65] and the Br. Minister[66] were absent—The Diplomats did not spare their remarks on the Slidell-Mason business—I told one of them as they were so partial to the British mode of doing business, I hope

[63] In early November 1861, Capt. Charles Wilkes commanding *San Jacinto*, stopped and boarded *Trent*, a British mail steamer, and removed two Confederate diplomats bound for Europe, James Murray Mason and John Sliddell. The action caused an international incident as Wilkes had acted in violation of international law by removing the two from a neutral vessel. Wilkes discussed the episode in his autobiography; see *Autobiography of Rear Admiral Charles Wilkes, U.S. Navy 1798–1877*, ed. William James Morgan, et al. (Washington, DC: Naval History Division, 1978), 767–81.

[64] The trip took place on 27 December 1861. Earl Schenk Miers and C. Percy Powell, *Lincoln Day by Day: A Chronology 1809–1865* (Dayton, OH: Morningside, 1991), 85.

[65] William Henry Seward.

[66] Lord Lyons; Richard Bickerton Pemell Lyons.

before long they would have some further experience of it—it has since turned out so—bitterly enough—The Prince de J. was there & the French Minister—but they avoided meeting

1862

New Years day came (1862) and the usual forms followed,—but there was no real gaiety—we Americans were too much concerned to be at ease—The President was kind as usual shaking hands with all—Next day he was at my quarters in the Navy Yard—sat some while—and talked—but was not satisfied with affairs—speaking of one of the expeditions that was not ready—he observed with much feeling "no one is ready"

A few days later the *Pensacola* passed down the river under the fire of the reb. batteries but they did her no injury—[67]

Then came the unlooked for resignation of Cameron Sec. of War—he seemed in good spirits a few days afterwards at a dinner given by Hanseatic Minister—[68]

It was some relief to heavy apprehensions—the party of Mrs Lincoln—[69]It was [a] very elegant affair and most creditable to Mrs Lincoln—gathered in all the distinguished and a few more—and the presence of some two or three showed how singularly free was our good President from ill-feeling—one gentleman I noted who had been so far suspected at the beginning that he was provided for at Fort Lafayette—a lady too whose husband's door had been provided for a while with a Sentry—Fremont[70] was there Gen M^c^Clellan & family—and Gen

---

67 Dahlgren reported that Capt. Henry W. Morris and *Pensacola* passed the batteries, which fired nearly two dozen shots but did no damage. ORN 5: 16–17.

68 Simon Cameron, a Pennsylvania politician, served as Lincoln's first Secretary of War. Allegations of corruption and mismanagement of the war effort swirled around Cameron. By early 1862, many politicians and much of the public had lost faith in him, leading him to resign from the cabinet. Lincoln appointed him minister to Russia. Paul Kahan, *Amiable Scoundrel: Simon Cameron, Lincoln's Scandalous Secretary of War* (Lincoln, NE: Potomac Books, 2016), 206–14. Rudolf Mathias Schleiden was the Hanseatic minister.

69 Lincoln's wife was Mary Todd Lincoln. This "presidential reception" began on 5 February 1862. Dahlgren noted in his diary that McClellan "admired my sword very much; for, being in full uniform, I wore that presented by the Seventy-first." Dahlgrèn, *Memoir of John A. Dahlgren*, 355–56.

70 Maj. Gen. John Charles Frémont. Before the war, he had led expeditions to the West and ran as the presidential candidate for the Republican Party in 1856. Ezra J. Warner, *Generals in Blue: Lives of the Union Commanders* (Baton Rouge: Louisiana State University Press, 1964), 160–61.

_____ who a few days later was suddenly arrested on suspicion[71]—The supper was superb—Of course Mrs Lincoln was abused by all who had not been invited; but she did her part handsomely for all that—

Our kind President suffered a stinging blow by the death of his little boy Willie—[72]which saddened the appearance of better fortune—breaking out around us:—In the West Foote had opened the ball by taking Fort Henry, and Grant was beginning that career at Fort Donelson that was to end at Richmond—Burnside & Goldsborough had captured Roanoke I.—[73]

The President willing & anxious to use every opportunity of peace proclaims an Amnesty[74]—The 22[d]—served to inaugurate the Reb. President[75] and with us to remember Wash—Congress assembled to hear his farewell Address[76], and there was a vast gathering of notabilities—Domestic & foreign—The spectacle was very imposing—So tender still was the feeling to the South that the display of captured reb. flags was not permitted—they had been collected in the rotunda, & were not to enter the Hall,—

While preparation was being made on one part for an advance in full force upon the Rebel centre, a blow was struck directly at us, which was only warded off by the interposition of Providence—

On the 8th of March the rebel Ironclad *Merrimac* suddenly issued from the Elizabeth River, destroyed two of our frigates, and would have served all the

---

[71] As a result of the Ball's Bluff disaster, suspicion fell upon the loyalty of Brig. Gen. Charles Pomeroy Stone. On 8 February 1862 he was arrested and held in confinement until that August. No formal charges were filed and he was restored to command in May 1863. Stone resigned from the Army in 1864. Ibid., 480–81.

[72] Lincoln's son, William W. Lincoln, died on 20 February 1862.

[73] Capt. Andrew Hull Foote, commander of a naval flotilla on the western waters, captured Fort Henry on the Tennessee River on 6 February 1862. On 16 February, Brig. Gen. Ulysses S. Grant captured nearby Fort Donelson on the Cumberland River. The loss of these forts forced Confederates in the west to rearrange their troop dispositions and also made the Cumberland and Tennessee Rivers available for Union use. Flag Officer Louis M. Goldsborough, commander of the North Atlantic Blockading Squadron, and Brig. Gen. Ambrose Burnside captured Confederate-held Roanoke Island, NC. In the following campaign, Burnside moved his troops into the North Carolina interior.

[74] Presumably Lincoln's executive order of 14 February, where he ordered all political prisoners held by the military to be released, contingent on their not providing any further aid to the Confederates. Miers and Powell, *Lincoln Day by Day*, 95.

[75] On 22 February, Washington's birthday, Jefferson Davis was inaugurated as President of the Confederacy, previously having been only the provisional president.

[76] George Washington's "Farewell Address" of 19 September 1786. In it, he called for Americans to set aside differences and work for the preservation of the Union and the common welfare.

others present in the same way—[77]

Though it was Sunday I was sitting in the ordnance office attending to some public business that could not be postponed,—when the President was announced—I stept out to his carriage—"Get your hat and ride up with me,"—in a minute I was in the carriage by his side—"I have frightful news"—and then self-composed, though earnest he told of the *Merrimac*'s raid

Half an hour landed us at the White House,—In the cabinet were several of the Secretaries—Gen. McClellan &c after some desultory remarks all the telegrams were read carefully—discussion followed—then the President said to Gen. McClellan, Meigs & myself "Now you are a Committee to advise measures,"—just step into the next room and talk it over"—[78]The arrival of the *Monitor* however settled the matter and the *Merrimac* was sealed up for the remainder of her term—

The mission of the *Merrimac* having thus failed, the rebel army evacuated Manassas and drew back on their Capital, for they seemed to be better informed of the meditated flank move of McClellan than our own public

The effect of this change was magical upon affairs at Washington—the throng of officers vanished from the hotels and the streets—the rebel batteries on the river were abandoned and the tide of War seemed rolled entirely away from us—

A few days later the President & Secs. of War[79] & State went down to Alex. to see Gen. McClellan—I sent up a messenger to let him know and he came down—dressed plainly and without ceremony or attendance—a pleasant conversation ensued in the Cabin about matters generally—then the Gen. landed and

[77] CSS *Virginia*, a Confederate ironclad built on the hull of the steam frigate *Merrimack*, sortied on 8 March 1862, sinking both *Congress* and *Cumberland.*

[78] This conference took place on 9 March 1862. After the war, Gideon Welles recalled "that day and its incidents were among the most unpleasant and uncomfortable of my life." Lincoln brought Dahlgren to the White House, where Lincoln, Stanton, Seward, Welles, Assistant Secretary of War Watson, Brig. Gen. Montgomery C. Meigs, McClellan, and Lincoln's aide John G. Nicolay waited. After discussion, Lincoln directed Dahlgren, McClellan, and Meigs to make arrangements to block the Potomac by sinking ships full of stones and gravel to protect against a raid on Washington by CSS *Virginia*. Dahlgren asked Welles on both 10 and 11 March to take command of *Monitor* as its captain, Cmdr. Worden, had been disabled. Welles refused. Ultimately, about 60 canal boats were prepared to serve as blockships, but the duel between *Monitor* and CSS *Virginia* abated the threat to Washington. Dahlgren, *Memoir of John A. Dahlgren*, 358–60; William E. Gienapp and Erica L. Gienapp, eds., *The Civil War Diary of Gideon Welles, Lincoln's Secretary of the Navy: The Original Manuscript Edition*, (Urbana: The Knox College Lincoln Studies Center and the University of Illinois Press, 2014), 679–81.

[79] Edwin M. Stanton replaced Simon Cameron as the Secretary of War.

we returned to the Navy Yard—[80]

The move for the Peninsula is now fairly afoot—the Potomac is crowded with every description of vessel carrying troops, horses, field guns—stores of all kinds—the President is constantly on the move, looking with deepest interest at the proceedings—

Early in May, our army overcame the resistance at Yorktown and moved up the Peninsula,—came the news at the same time that our fleet had taken New Orleans[81]

About the middle of May—some of the Cabinet visited M^c^Clellan at Cumberland on the Pamunkey I was with them–a large corps of the Army here, about to move upon Richmond—M^c^Clellan came on board, with many officers,—also the Prince de J. and his nephews—matters were discussed—weather rainy & uncomfortable—We left soon after,—looked at Yorktown, and at Norfolk, and at all that was to be seen of the redoubtable *Merrimac*—which was little more than the lip of her stern pushing above water,—the rest lay below on the bottom—[82]

Then we followed up the James—saw the batteries abandoned by the rebels—and further on encountered a double-ender coming down—reported the fight at Drury bluff—*Galena* severely damaged—There I passed on, intending to

---

80 This trip took place on 18 March. Though not mentioned here, Assistant Secretary of the Navy Gustavus Vasa Fox accompanied Lincoln, Seward, Stanton, and Dahlgren. During the meeting, the men discussed war plans and McClellan also urged the promotion of Burnside to major general, not realizing that Burnside had already been promoted. Dahlgren, *Memoir of John A. Dahlgren*, 361.

81 The Confederates opposing McClellan's army left their defenses around Yorktown on the night of 3 May; the Union Army took Yorktown the following day. In April, David G. Farragut bombarded the Confederate defenses below New Orleans; his ships passed the Confederate batteries and captured the city on 29 April. Several days later, on 1 May, Union Army forces under Maj. Gen. Benjamin F. Butler occupied the city.

82 On 13 May 1862, Dahlgren joined Welles, Stanton, Attorney General Edward Bates, and other "ladies and gentleman" aboard the steamer *Baltimore* to visit McClellan at Cumberland Landing on the Pamunkey River. Bates recorded in his diary that the party included Welles, Welles's wife and niece, Seward, Seward's son Frederick, Bates's wife, Commodore Goldsborough, Goldsborough's wife and daughter, Chief of the U.S. Navy Bureau of Medicine and Surgery William Whelan, Chief Clerk of the Navy William Faxon, Eva Dahlgren, as well as other relatives of the party. The Prince de Joinville and his nephews, Louis Philippe, comte de Paris, and Robert, duc de Chartres, served as aides to McClellan. The trip lasted several days, with the visit to Yorktown on 15 May, Norfolk on 16 May, and Jamestown Island on 17 May. Dahlgren, *Memoir of John A. Dahlgren*, 366–67; *The Diary of Edward Bates 1859–1866*, ed. Howard K. Beale (Washington, DC: Government Printing Office, 1933), 258–59, 259n.

Galena after the engagement at Drewry's Bluff. Visible are two IX-inch Dahlgren guns, and just left of bottom center, a bung plugs a hole from the battle. Photograph, 1862.

Naval History and Heritage Command, Photographic Collections, NH 53984.

go as high as the bluff,—but the Sec. of State could not spare the time[83]—When I visited the *Galena*, it was evident that she had been fairly at her work, and that Rodgers had not withdrawn her any too soon—in fact she was well mauled—[84]

On the 23rd of May the President rode through Fredericksburg—on horse-

83 Dahlgren wrote in his diary that at 4 a.m. on 18 May, Seward "wanted to move for Washington right off. There were State reasons for it." *Baltimore* arrived back at the Washington Navy Yard on 19 May. Dahlgren, *Memoir of John A. Dahlgren*, 368.

84 Cmdr. John Rodgers, of *Galena*, had engaged Confederate land batteries at Drewry's Bluff on the James, along with several other vessels. According to Rodgers, during the battle *Galena* "expended nearly all her ammunition." After the action, Rodgers reported that "we demonstrated that" the ironclad "is not shot-proof" and thought that "the *Galena* should be repaired before sending her to sea." Of her crew, 13 were killed and 11 wounded. ORN 7: 357–58.

back attended by Gen McDowell and staff—Secr. of War & myself in company, generally the houses were shut—but we carried our own welcome—the force here was about 45000 men—and the review showed them to be in fine order—all ready to advance and give a hand to McClellan at Hanover junction[85]

Next morning about daylight we landed at the Navy Yard wharf—just as the President crossed the plank from the boat a telegram was handed him—he said good morning to me, stepped into his carriage with the Sec of War and drove off—

There was matter enough in that slip of paper—it announced the onslaught of Jackson at Harper's Ferry—and of course spread rapidly—my share was a telegram asking if I could send my Howitzers to Harper F—I offered beside to send some heavy Cannon and that evening they and the Howitzers with a choice body of seamen were being whirled on the Railway to the Ferry—where they arrived in good season and were soon planted in a commanding position some 2000 feet above the ocean level—the only officer I could spare was a young master and his associate was my son Ulric, who was now to begin the career for his country that only ended with his life—[86]

To this battery, opened in good time on Jackson's columns, the safety of the post was probably due—the rebs were astonished at shells as large as the IX^inch making havoc among them, and drew off—It was Thursday late at night that Ulric Dahlgren came to the War Depart. with an account of the repulse—The President & Sec of War listened with interest and the young man returned with an appointment as Captain—[87]

We were now to pass the trying ordeal of the campaign in the Peninsula—of course it is needless for me to go over the well told tale—

---

[85] Dahlgren left for Aquia Landing with Lincoln and Stanton late in the evening on 22 May. Details on the visit can be found in Dahlgren, *Memoir of John A. Dahlgren*, 369–70.

[86] The Naval Battery, under the command of Acting Master Charles H. Daniels, arrived at Harper's Ferry on 27 May to support Brig. Gen. Rufus Saxton's command. Ulric Dahlgren also accompanied it as a volunteer aide-de-camp. The battery was in place by 28 May, when it "had some splendid practice . . . shelling the woods and heights across the Shenandoah." On 30 May, the battery helped repel a Confederate attack. Saxton wrote: "I cannot speak too highly of the services of Lieutenant Daniels, U.S. Volunteers, and his splendid rifled 9-inch Dahlgren. Both he and they did their work well." He later noted that the "naval battery of Dahlgren guns on Maryland Heights, 2,000 feet above the level of the sea, did splendid service throughout the entire siege." OR 12: 1, 634, 636, 641.

[87] Ulric Dahlgren met with Lincoln and Stanton on 29 May; John Dahlgren later wrote that "what the lad had to say was of interest, and was clearly narrated, both to the President and to Secretary Stanton." As Ulric left, Lincoln "tendered . . . an appointment as additional aide-de-camp, with the rank of captain." Dahlgren, *Memoir of Ulric Dahlgren*, 63.

On the 10th of July the President landed at the Navy Yard—he was just from the army of the James—anxious, and harassed by the fierce conflict of opinions about him, he left so privately that the public knew not of it—reached the army, heard and saw for himself—I gave him refreshments at my quarters—he told me there were 81,000 men present and in fine condition for battle—

July 18th (1862) I was commissioned as Chief of Bureau of Ordnance—and therefore detached from command of the Navy Yard—a change by no means acceptable to me, but I had no choice the Dept. had permitted me to refuse a year ago, but now insisted—

The Commission as Chief of Bureau was dated 18th July—and addressed to me as a Commander—So I was the first of the grade that ever filled the office,—and when I declined it a year ago perhaps the only officer who ever declined such a position

And so ended a service of one year and three months as Commandant of the Washington Navy Yard—which came to me not by the ordinary routine, but the unexpected and extraordinary events of the Rebellion—In that situation it had been my fortune to be so associated with the great passing events and the actors, as will never occur again—For surely the Country will never again be called to pass through such an ordeal—it is the last time that the people of any section will ever appeal from the ballot to the sword and bayonet—I was also fortunate in not being transferred from the Yard until its temporary importance was at an end

It was my good fortune while in that command to receive a practical proof of appreciation, in the enactment of a Law to enable me to retain the command,—for being only a Commander I was thereby disabled—

It is true that I did not desire to go to the Bureau,—but only because in such circumstances I wished more active duty.

The duties of the Bureau now brought me in connection with all the Navy Yards and Foundries of cannon &c—The latter part of July I found it necessary to look personally at our new Ironclad the *Ironsides* at Philad.—and the Monitors at New York, where I had an interview with their distinguished Inventor—though my attention had been long given to him—from his essay with the *Princeton*, and he always had my hearty admiration, as a man of real genius—[88]

The rebs. are now busy with their ironclads for the *Merrimac* had certainly been a success,—As it would take time for us to build I was anxious to resort meanwhile to temporary expedients—among others to cut down the *Niagara*

[88] Swedish inventor John Ericsson designed both *Princeton* and *Monitor*.

John Ericsson, the Swedish engineer who designed *Princeton*, also designed the famed *Monitor*. Photograph of print.

Library of Congress, Prints and Photographs Division, Detroit Publishing Company Collection, LC-DIG-det-4a26414.

and fill her with Steam power, for a Ram-Ally.[89] 4th I received promotion to be a Captain by appointment, dated back to 16th July—

The city once more in commotion—the Rebel General taking advantage of the withdrawal of McClellan is concentrating on Pope, and news are coming in of disaster—[90]

On the 19th the President sent for me on official business,—and afterwards began to talk of the "situation"—ending with the remark "now I am to have a sweat of it for 5 or 6 days"—

By the first of Septr. it was well enough known that results were discouraging—our army falling back, in as good order as a beaten army could—but fighting bravely—Fresh levies coming through the city from the North brings back the sights of previous days—the Army too is much distressed and even Clerks are

[89] *Niagara* was decommissioned on 16 June 1862. She underwent a refit including new boilers and armament. Paul H. Silverstone, *Civil War Navies* 1855–1883 (Annapolis, MD: Naval Institute Press, 2001), 17–18.

[90] Emboldened by McClellan's retrograde maneuver to Harrison's Landing, Confederate Gen. Robert E. Lee began shifting his army northward. His Army of Northern Virginia would clash with Maj. Gen. John Pope's army on 29–30 August 1862 at Second Bull Run, which resulted in a Union loss and Pope's men falling back on Washington.

sent from the city to aid the wounded—I forwarded men from the Ordnance for the same purpose—

Really I did not consider the city in danger if the troops were handled rightly,—for we had the men of the Peninsula and other veterans,—who would not be brushed out of a strong position—In the great stir of such events, it was impossible to trace the minor atoms of the mass, and I was much concerned about my son Ully—of whom I heard little,—but at last an old seaman of the Ordnance who had been tending the wounded came to me,—while so engaged Ulric was riding by with his orderly, when spying his old friend he halted to greet him—he was not hurt though frequently in the melée, and though much fagged was hearty—A day or two afterwards he suddenly entered my office—the brave boy looked as cheerful as ever,—but had worn off every ounce of spare flesh,—bronzed as a veteran—Passing out of the Department, we came full on the President who stopped and greeted us with that warm kindness, so much his own—But how anxious and wasted—Still the pleasant smile lighted his face as he spoke, and he motioned us to the War Depart—and drawing Ulric by the arm, just inside of its outer door,—he said—"Come now tell me what you have seen"—the young soldier clearly and distinctly told of the last battles, on which doubts had arisen—while the President leaning forward lost not a word—and yielded to some absorbing thought when the narration was ended Then he shook hands, bade Ully come and see him & pursued his way to the White House How little either imagined that both were to fall by the hands of bitter enemies!—

The middle of Septem found the enemy in Maryland, hoping to raise the standard of revolt there,—but McClellan was close upon him, and on the 14th the sound of Cannon heard in Wash$^{n.}$ gave token that the issue was joined—[91]

Early in Nov. the first of the new Monitors (*Passaic*) is ready for trial and I proceeded to New York to look after the Ordnance part of the vessel;[92] the noise of the XI^{in} is very stunning

A few days afterwards while in my office, received a telegram saying that Ulric had been captured in a dash into Fredericksburg—and I passed a troubled night—but better news came next day—he had surprised the place,—entered it

[91] Confederate Gen. Robert E. Lee and the Army of Northern Virginia invaded Maryland in early September 1862. On 14 September, Union forces under Maj. Gen. George B. McClellan engaged in three separate battles in an attempt to take control of the passes through South Mountain, in Frederick County, MD, and thereby threaten Lee's dispersed forces and prevent the concentration of the Confederate Army. The Union attacks were largely unsuccessful, and three days later the Union and Confederate Armies met in battle at Antietam.

[92] The *Passaic*-class monitors moved the pilothouse to the top of the turret and were armed with one XI-inch and one XV-inch smoothbore cannon; Silverstone, *Civil War Navies*, 5.

with some 60 or 70 cavalry,—and after a series of continued conflicts, hand to hand with rebel cavalry, had routed three times his number, and was in possession—finally he came out with prisoners more than half his command. It was bravely done, and his own notion.[93]

The Winter season brought Congress together,—and then came the fatal battle of Fredericksburg—[94]

[93] A thorough discussion of Ulric Dahlgren's 9 November raid and safe return on 10 November 1862, as well as transcriptions of the various dispatches referred to above, is found in Dahlgren, *Memoir of Ulric Dahlgren*, 92–116.

[94] From 11–13 December 1862, Confederate Gen. Robert E. Lee repelled an attack by Maj. Gen. Ambrose Burnside, delivering a heavy defeat to the Army of the Potomac.

CHAPTER 4

Promotion, Command of the South Atlantic Blockading Squadron, and the Siege of Charleston, 1863

1863

Early in Febr. I encountered the President entering the Navy Depart.—he said that Mr Seward had told him of a raid by rebel Rams from Charleston, and he had come over to hear more about it.[1]

Feb. 12—Congress puts vote of thanks to Commo. Stringham, Captain

[1] On 31 January 1863, the Confederate ironclad rams CSS *Chicora* and CSS *Palmetto State* attacked the South Atlantic Blockading Squadron outside of Charleston. The Confederate vessels forced the surrender of *Mercedita*, although they did not take her as a prize, and inflicted heavy damage upon *Keystone State*. ORN 13: 577–99; Robert M. Browning Jr., *Success Is All that Was Expected: The South Atlantic Blockading Squadron During the Civil War* (Washington, DC: Brassey's, 2002), 138–43. News of the attack reached Washington around 4 February; Gideon Welles recorded in his diary that "we have the whole world agog with an account of an onset on our fleet before Charleston." Secretary of State William Seward evinced concern over the attack, as foreign consuls in Charleston declared that the attack had lifted the blockade. William E. Gienapp and Erica L. Gienapp, eds., *The Civil War Diary of Gideon Welles, Lincoln's Secretary of the Navy: The Original Manuscript Edition* (Urbana: The Knox College Lincoln Studies Center and the University of Illinois Press, 2014), 134,134n.

Stephen C. Rowan.
Glass negative, c. 1863.

Brady Photograph Collection, National Archives, B-4517.

Davis, myself Rowan and Porter—[2]

On the last day of Febr. I learn that my nomination as Rear Admiral has been confirmed by the Senate—

On the 4th of March Congress adjourned and closed its existence—Perhaps no body of men ever were charged with greater responsibilities—I was on the

[2] On 11 July, Lincoln recommended that Congress thank the mentioned officers, among others. On 7 February, Congress approved a joint resolution: "That the thanks of Congress be, and are hereby, given to the following officers of the United States Navy, upon the recommendation of the President of the United States, viz: Commodore Charles Henry Davis, for distinguished services in conflict with the enemy at Fort Pillow, at Memphis, and for successful operations at other points in the waters of the Mississippi River: Captain John A. Dahlgren, for distinguished service in the line of his profession, improvements in ordnance, and zealous and efficient labors to the ordnance branch of service: Captain Stephen C. Rowan, for distinguished services in the waters of North Carolina, and particularly in the capture of Newbern, being in chief command of the naval forces: Commander David D. Porter, for the bravery and skill displayed in the attack on the post of Arkansas, which surrendered to the combined military and naval forces on the tenth of January, eighteen hundred and sixty-three: Rear-Admiral Silas H. Stringham, now on the retired list, for distinguished services in the capture of Forts Hatteras and Clark: and that a copy of that resolution be forwarded to each of the above officers by the President of the United States." *Acts and Resolutions of the Third Session of the Thirty-Seventh Congress, begun on Monday, December 1, 1862 and Ended on Wednesday, March 4, 1863* (Washington, DC: Government Printing Office, 1863), 238–39. For the text of Lincoln's recommendation, see *Complete Works of Abraham Lincoln,* New and Enlarged Edition, ed. John G. Nicolay and John Hay (n.p.: Lincoln Memorial University, 1894), Volume 7: 267–68.

floor there was nothing of the confusion that too often discredits such occasions.—but quiet—and the mere form of proceeding—Presently the Speaker[3] rose,—and so did every member,—he made a short address and then announced that the 37th Congress was dissolved—

The President is evidently much occupied in thought with Charleston—The ironclads are there and Dupont is to operate before long, but when, is not known exactly—[4]

Among the measures of the late Congress was the Act incorporating the "National Academy of Science"—consisting of 50 members, styled Incorporators—of which I was named as one—but as soon as it was organised, I sent a resignation to the President of the Academy (Prof. Bache)[5] who replied next day (May 15th) regretting that I had done so, and urged me not to insist,—but I felt under the circumstances that it was best to do so and therefore wrote again, adhering to my determination—The honor was duly appreciated and quite a temptation but it is not allowable to occupy such position without contributing to the work and I felt that my hands & head were fully occupied with public duties.—For similar reasons I had also withdrawn from the American Association[6] &c—formerly.

Towards the end of March I observed that the President seem rather discouraged at the state of affairs,—more so than I had ever seen before—It was pretty well understood that the new ironclads would soon be tried at Charleston and public expectation was alive

In this state of affairs I left Wash. to visit our Naval posts in the West and look to the Arrangements for arming the ironclads building at Pittsburgh, Cincinnati, St Louis &c—in the course of this tour I had an opportunity of realising the immense capabilities of this great section of the Union—While at Cairo came

3 Galusha A. Grow (R-PA).

4 Rear Adm. Samuel Francis Du Pont commanded the South Atlantic Blockading Squadron and had been instructed to make an attack on Charleston. Du Pont feared that his ironclads alone would be unable to deal with Confederate defenses and urged for a joint operation rather than a strictly naval effort. Both Welles and Fox, however, pushed for an attack and believed Du Pont to be too cautious. In early 1863, a number of new monitors arrived at Port Royal to strengthen Du Pont's squadron in preparation for the attack. Kevin J. Weddle, *Lincoln's Tragic Admiral: The Life of Samuel Francis Du Pont* (Charlottesville: University of Virginia Press, 2005), 154–86.

5 The National Academy of Sciences was established on 3 March 1863, with Alexander Dallas Bache as its first president. Bache succeeded Ferdinand Rudolph Hassler as superintendant of the United States Coastal Survey in 1843, in which post he served until his death in 1867.

6 The American Association for the Advancement of Science.

A stereo view of the turret of the monitor *Passaic*. The turret armor shows battle damage from cannonballs. Stereo view by Samuel A. Cooley, c. 1863.

Robin G. Stanford Collection, Library of Congress, Prints and Photographs Division, LC-DIG-stereo-1s04456.

tidings of the attack on Charleston—and its want of success—On the 20th April I reached Wash$^{n.}$ and found the affairs at Charleston occupied much attention in doors and out—The public will not be content with anything but success,—though experience should have taught them not to ask for impossibilities—[7]

A few days afterwards while sitting in my office the President after reading the last telegrams aloud, observed that he had written a joint letter to the General and Admiral &c[8]

And now Hooker[9] is about to put his army in motion in obedience to the cry of "<u>On to Richmond</u>"—but there has been a check on the publicity of our Military operations,—and the enemy does not so readily learn of them from our

7 On 7 April 1863, a fleet of Union ironclads under Du Pont attacked Confederate fortifications at Charleston Harbor. The bombardment inflicted little damage and revealed shortcomings of the monitors. Du Pont had warned against the folly of the attack, believing correctly that Confederate defenses, particularly submarine obstructions, were too strong for the Union fleet. Ibid., 187–98.

8 Lincoln wrote both Maj. Gen. David Hunter and Du Pont on 14 April 1863, instructing them to cooperate at Charleston, advising that they continue their demonstrations against the Confederates. He also wanted them to attempt to capture Charleston, "if it affords any considerable chance of success." OR 14: 441.

9 Maj. Gen. Joseph Hooker received command of the Army of the Potomac after the Battle of Fredericksburg; he spent much of early 1863 reorganizing the army and preparing it for the 1863 campaigns. As with every other commander of the Army of the Potomac, he faced intense pressure from the public and politicians to capture the Confederate capital of Richmond.

own Press: so in general there is nothing flitting but rumors—first his crossing and then of battle,—but not of victory—this is generally understood by the 4th of May and each day tells something of detail but still not all,—On the 6th the papers were announcing victory in large headings when a two words by telegraph from my son told me distinctly that the army had recrossed, for it was dated "Hd. qrs. at Falmouth"—He had been in the thickest and lost his horse[10]

Capt. Drayton came in—just from Charleston—bringing home the monitor *Passaic*—he says it would be madness to go into Charleston again—which, as brave and able a man as he would not say without good reason.[11]

On the 20th May I was in New York with the Assist. Secretary and visited the *Passaic* with Adm. Gregory and Capt. Ericsson—she was out of water, on the Railway, so we went round and examined and discussed—then visited the *Puritan* and *Dictator*—Ericsson a great engineer—[12]

When I came back to Washn. found much gossip afloat in Naval circles about affairs at Charleston—it is rumored that Adm. Dupont will be relieved,—successor not determined on, though opinion points to Adm. Foote—And so it proved shortly after—for one evening Foote came to my house to urge me to go with him—Naturally I had a great disinclination to go afloat except in full command yet I was anxious for sea service but I finally yielded to the wishes of the Navy Department and of Foote—So it was arranged that I should command the Ironclads of the Fleet separately and have the priviledge of entering Charleston Harbor whenever it was ordered[13]

---

[10] Hooker had crossed the Rappahannock and Rapidan Rivers at the end of April. His army fought the Army of Northern Virginia under Gen. Robert E. Lee from 1 May to 3 May 1863, and suffered a crushing loss during the Chancellorsville campaign.

[11] During the attack at Charleston, *Passaic*, under the command of Capt. Percival Drayton, suffered mishaps and damage. One of its guns had been disabled early and its turret jammed after being struck by enemy fire. The pilot house had also been severely damaged. Drayton thought that "the pilot house is not capable of withstanding heavy shot for any length of time, and even throws a doubt on the turret itself, or at least its machinery." ORN 14:11.

[12] Assistant Secretary of the Navy Gustavus Vasa Fox and Rear Adm. Francis H. Gregory. Both *Puritan* and *Dictator* were Ericsson-designed monitors then building in New York. The former had been laid down in 1862 and was of a single-turret design, while the latter was laid down in 1863 and was to bear two turrets. *Dictator* was never finished. Paul H. Silverstone, *Civil War Navies* 1855–1883 (Annapolis, MD: Naval Institute Press, 2001), 8–9.

[13] Welles ordered Foote to relieve Du Pont and also requested that Dahlgren serve as second-in-command. Dahlgren, for his part, suggested that the fleet attacking Charleston be embodied as a command separate from the South Atlantic Blockading Squadron. During a meeting in New York City with Foote, Dahlgren received command of the ironclads of the fleet. Robert J. Schneller Jr., *A Quest for Glory: A Biography of Rear Admiral John A. Dahlgren* (Annapolis, MD: Naval Institute Press, 1996), 243.

Major General Quincy A. Gillmore. Glass negative, c. 1865.

Brady Photograph Collection, National Archives, B-3323.

On the 3rd of June I was in N. York to confer with Adm. Foote and found him not at all well,—complained of a head ache which however I knew he had always been liable to when we were messmates—Whilst conversing Gen. Gilmore came in, who I understood was to conduct the operations by land—we were introduced but exchanged only a few words, as he had business with Adm Foote, and as not having yet received my formal orders, I drew off to another part of the room and entered into conversation with Gen. Strong, leaving Gen. Gillmore to confer privately with Adm. Foote.[14]

Next day I returned to Washington—soon after came the tidings of the Cavalry fight at Beverly Ford, where Hooker anticipating mischief had promptly let loose his horsemen on the rebels:—it was very handsomely carried out, and I learned that my son Ulric with his habitual gallantry had accompanied the desperate charge of the Penn. Lancers[15] and had another narrow escape, for his horse was shot in several places—At Chancellorsville, he also lost his horse,—[16]Grant is striking heavy blows in the West—and will not be turned aside from his pur-

[14] Brig. Gen. George Strong, of Vermont, who would command a brigade sent to Charleston. He was wounded during the 18 July assault, contracted tetanus from the wound, and died several weeks later. Ezra J. Warner, *Generals in Blue: Lives of the Union Commanders* (Baton Rouge: Louisiana State University Press, 1964), 483–84.

[15] 6th Penn. Cav., also known as Rush's Lancers.

[16] For a description of the cavalry fight at Beverly Ford on 9 June 1863, see John A. Dahlgren, *Memoir of Ulric Dahlgren* (Philadelphia: J. B. Lippincott & Co., 1872), 147–51.

pose—[17] My eldest son was on this line, serving as Master in the Fleet—[18] So that all the men of my name North are in line of battle—

By the middle of June it is known positively that Lee taking advantage of the weakened state of our Army has marched Northward for Pennsylvania and soon after Hooker nothing daunted gallantly moves forward to attack the rebel Army—

About the 19th Adm. Foote was known to be lying ill at the Astor House, and having arrived the day before I went around immediately to see my friend—passed part of the morning and afternoon with him—conversing on our expedition—he was evidently very ill, and suffering from oppression at the chest—Next day he was unconscious,—I left him with most painful regret as business required my return—almost doubtful how his illness was to end—

Reached Washington and went to the Depart to make known the results of my journey,—the Depart. had other reports (Medical) of the condition of Adm. Foote—When I left, being Sunday I went to Church, and had not been there long when an official messenger from the Secretary required my attendance—I was then told that it would be impossible for Adm. Foote to go to Charleston, and that the command of the Naval forces in that quarter had been assigned to me—[19]

This was on the 22d June and on the 24th I left Washington for New York—to sail without delay for the South—

Thus ended my duty in the Bureau of Ordnance,—and indeed with Ordnance matters to this date—if ever at all to be resumed—it had nearly filled one year and during that time I not only administered the affairs of the Bureau, but also continued to conduct practical matters at my old Headquarters at the Navy Yard—remaining in the Navy Department until noon, then at the Ordn. Yard during the afternoon so that Uncle Sam could not complain of not getting the worth of what he paid me—

---

17 Maj. Gen. Ulysses S. Grant had renewed his operations to capture the Confederate stronghold at Vicksburg. He crossed the Mississippi River in April and fought several successful battles before besieging the Mississippi city in May 1863.

18 Charles B. Dahlgren had been appointed Acting Master on 14 May 1863. Edward W. Callahan, ed., *List of Officers of the Navy of the United States and of the Marine Corps from 1775 to 1900: Comprising a Complete Register of All Present and Former Commissioned, Warranted, and Appointed Officers of the United States Navy, and of the Marine Corps, Regular and Volunteer* (New York: L. R. Hammersly & Co., 1901), 146.

19 Foote suffered from Bright's disease, a chronic inflammation of the kidneys. This date was actually 21 June; 22 June was a Monday. Spencer C. Tucker, *Andrew Foote: Civil War Admiral on Western Waters* (Annapolis, MD: Naval Institute Press, 2000), 204.

The U.S. Fleet Offshore, from Morris Island, SC. Glass negative, Haas & Peale, 1863.
Library of Congress, Prints and Photographs Division, LC-DIG-cwpb-04757.

On the 24th I took leave at the Navy Depart. and by night was in New York Next day my first care was to visit my old and beloved friend Foote—alas! he was delirious—a few words recalled the fast departing senses—the wandering eye rested on me for a brief moment and he uttered my name distinctly—even remembering my boys—then he relapsed and another day ended in this world the life of as brave and as good a man as ever served any country—no one better knew his virtues than I—no one prized them more dearly—we had been bosom friends for 20 years—and never a cloud between us—What a loss to the country!—[20]

But I was not allowed to linger over this sorrow—I was to leave at once and the vessel that was to take me was yet to be purchased,—for a regular War vessel was not to be had—However it was finally decided to buy a small screw steamer from a packet line—which was done and in the most hurried manner I left N. York on the 30th of June—without a staff officer, except Capt Badger[21] as Ordn. Officer of the Fleet or any domestics—in fact with less equipment than would bring a midshipman to meeting—which I would never advise any one to do that can help it—

[20] Foote died on 26 June. Observers blamed Foote's service on the western waters for breaking his health and causing his death. Ibid., 204.

[21] Lt. Cmdr. Oscar C. Badger.

"*Patapsco* engaging Sullivans Id. Batteries," 6 April 1863. Drawing on paper, Alfred R. Waud or William Waud, 1863.

Morgan collection of Civil War drawings, Library of Congress, Prints and Photographs Division, LC-DIG-ppmsca-21438.

The run Southerly was present—On the 4th of July we were off Port Royal and anchored there about breakfast time—found Adm. Dupont in the *Wabash*, (blue flag at the Main—) with several vessels of the squadron—The Admiral sent me a very kind note,—saying he would send his barge for me at 10^{OC}—going aboard, the Admiral met me at the gangway, and the deck was alive with officers, marines and men—according to the ceremonial of the service—few men are endowed with the superb personal presence of Dupont—and the equipment of the ship was in full accord with the high condition of the best days of the Navy—chiefly due to the fine abilities of her commander Capt. Raymond Rodgers[22]—the officers were regular & of high stamp—one who has not seen a U.S. ship of War in the pride of full efficiency can form no idea from description of what it is—

In the conference that followed with the Admiral he apprised me that Gen. Gillmore had addressed him asking for aid to operate against Morris. I.—[23] but that as he knew of my coming, he preferred not to act—In the afternoon I went ashore and Gen. Gilmore then explained his plans and asked for an immediate move—though the whole subject was so new to me—the locality I had never seen,—nor did I know anything of the force to be handed over, I acceded at

[22] As indicated, Du Pont's flagship at this time was *Wabash*, and his fleet captain was Christopher Raymond Perry Rodgers.

[23] Gillmore's proposals for joint operations, and Du Pont's response, are found in ORN 14: 298–99, 304, and 307–8. Du Pont made a note on the latter request from Gillmore that he had discussed the matter with Dahlgren on 4 July 1863, ORN 14: 308.

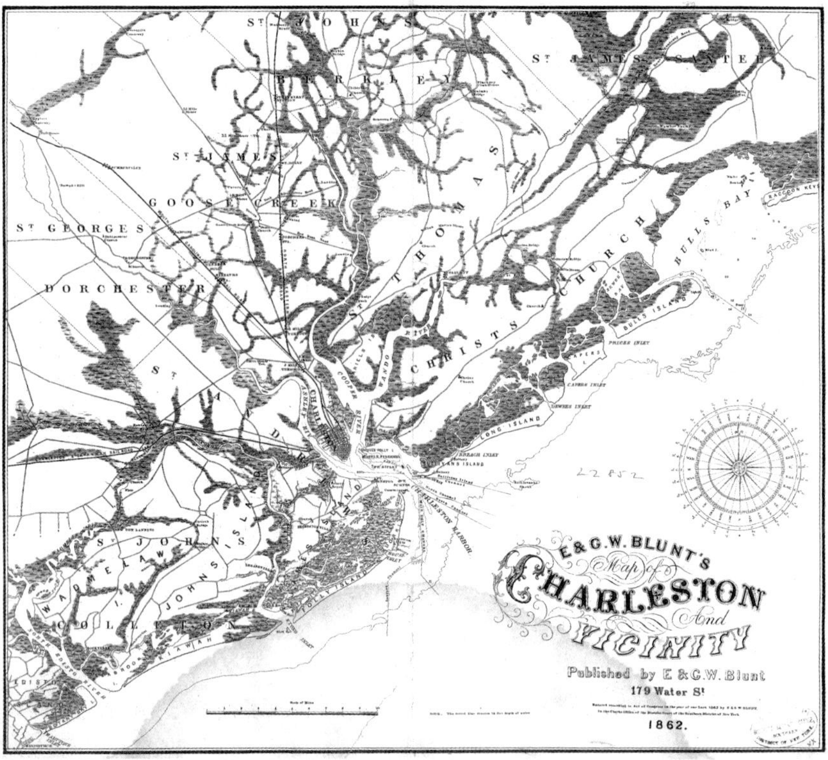

"E. & G. W. Blunt's Map of Charleston and vicinity." Map, 1862.

Library of Congress, Geography and Map Division, g3914c.cw0369000.

once and the General named Wednesd^{y}—the difficulties that lay in my way were—that three of the Monitors were in the hands of the mechanics being strengthened in the parts that proved weak in the attack of 7th April,—[24] this work must be discontinued and the vessels got ready in some way or the other;—all the arrangements for movement and battle were to be made,—I had not even seen the locality, nor had time to study it—and had yet to form a staff—I was entirely without instructions except to take command of the squadron,—though it has been asserted since that a regular plan had been agreed on and in my possession—which is entirely false—the Naval attack was made on my own respon-

[24] Du Pont's attempt on Charleston had revealed that the monitors suffered from too little armor on the decks, turrets, and pilothouses. *Nahant, Montauk*, and *Weehawken* had been repairing at the time Dahlgren arrived. ORN 14: 317.

sibility and I so informed the Department in my first dispatch—[25]

On the day before that agreed on Gen. G. asked me to postpone for one day,—he was not ready—I agreed—

Wednes. morn. left Port Royal and reached Charleston bar by night—before daylight of Thursday—the Monitors which I had ordered were off the bar and I was preparing to go on board of one when an Aid came from the General asking another postponement for one day—he was not ready—

Finally on Friday morning the work began—the batteries on Folly I. opened

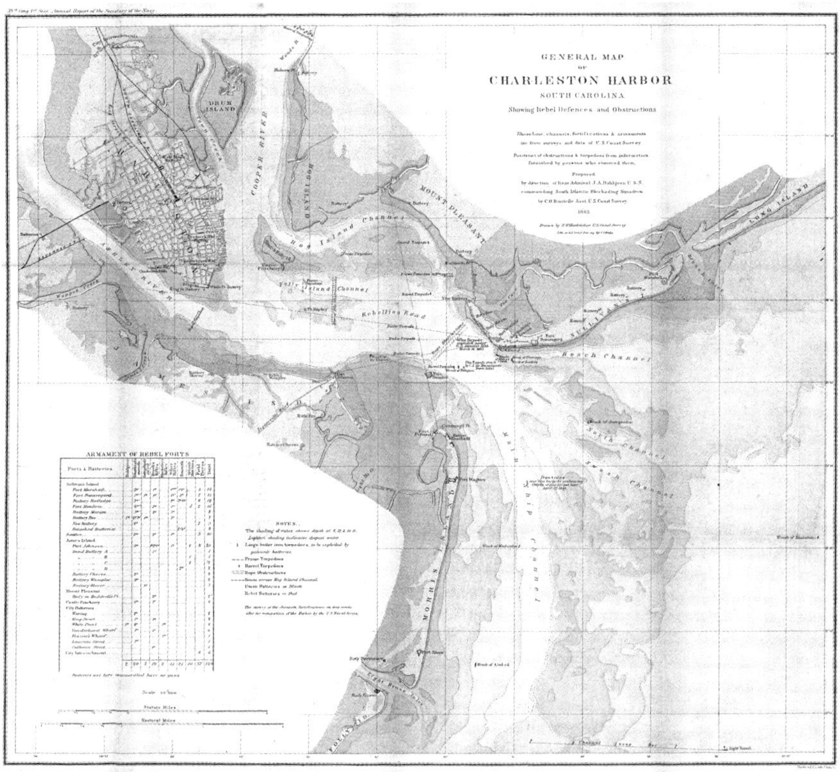

"General Map of Charleston Harbor South Carolina Showing Rebel Defences and Obstructions." Prepared by the U.S. Coast Survey at the direction of Rear Admiral John A. Dahlgren. From the 1865 *Report of the Secretary of the Navy*, 39th Congress 1st Session. Map, C. O. Boutelle and E[ugene] Willenbacher, U.S. Coast Survey.

Library of Congress, Geography and Map Division, g3912c.cw0370100.

25 JAD: "See first dispatch to Navy Dep in report of Sec. Navy." Printed in ORN 14:311.

a rapid and steady fire,—and I, standing across the bar with four Monitors ranged up and began a flanking fire—[26]the effect of which was instantly noticeable—the rebels disconcerted by it—began to waver, then to slacken, the fire which they returned to the land battery, and at last to break—by this time our troops were landing and the rebels abandoned their works quickly, fleeing up the island

Seeing this I steamed the Monitors in the same direction and presently laid my own Monitor abreast of Fort Wagner and opened fire on it—The other Monitors followed me in line of battle—[27]the action continued until noon, but no further effort was made by the General, although it was plain that this was the auspicious moment,—the enemy being beaten and in confusion,—after giving the seamen their dinner I resumed the attack, and continued to batter the work until 6^{PM} when I hauled off—The first part of the day had been a brilliant success ending in the capture of all the Southern defences—but the failure to follow it up by an assault lost us the fruits—The statement since made by the General is that his men were fatigued,—true it was a hot day in July—but it was the early part of the day and only nine O.C. in the morning when the Southern works were in our possession and the advance within range of Wagner—if the soldiers who had crossed were fatigued,—they might have been refreshed in two or three hours, and led forward,—or fresh other troops might have been brought over from Folly I—and pushed forward—in either case if ever Wagner was to be assaulted that was the time for it—

The work of the day acquainted me with some points of the Monitors, the endurance was capital,—my own vessel had been struck 67 times but the ponderous XV^{in} was too slow in repeating fire,—which was its own fault and not that of the Monitor and a fatal defect in hammering earth works, for which rapid fire is needed—their batteries being iron were fouled so as to reduce their speed—

If the Monitors had not been present on this occasion, the rebel Ironclads lying in Charleston harbor would have come down and operated on our troops with a flanking fire—which must have prevented the landing and the capture of the southern defences—and yet Gen G. asserts in his official [report][28] that the

26 *Catskill, Montauk, Nahant*, and *Weehawken*.

27 Dahlgren wrote and crossed out here the sentence: "The General appeared to halt his men as they came near the work."

28 In his report, Gillmore mentioned little about the assistance of the Navy. OR 28,1:8–12.

work could have been [carried] without the Navy[29]—which is not only untrue but unmanly to say after being thus assisted[30]—Nothing but the presence of the Monitors restrained the rebel ironclads; they had been out not long before and scattered our wooden vessels right & left—

The next morning an assault was made on Wagner—and without any notice to me,—as a consequence our soldiers went forward without the aid of the Naval fire—and were easily repulsed with severe loss—[31]The day previous the assault might have been made in force on a reduced and disheartened garrison, kept well down by the fire of the ironclads—instead of which it was made the day after upon a reinforced garrison, which had had time to collect its senses, and without the aid of the Naval fire—

The day after Gen. Gillmore came to see me—and seemed undecided what course to pursue—afterwards it appears that he concluded to try another assault covered by land batteries as well as by the Naval fire—batteries were accordingly established as quickly [as] possible and on the 15th a good spring tide and smooth sea enabled me to have the *Ironsides* gotten across the bar—

The day before the Gen. had informed me of his conclusion to try another assault on the 16th—when he expected to have 18 rifled guns in battery & 12 or

---

29 JAD: "Gen. Gillmore in a letter to me—July 7th—which is omitted from the correspondence with me says:—'It seems so important and in fact indispensable that the main ship channel abreast of Morris I. should be held against any attempt to dislodge us from that island, when once there, by the enemy's ironclads from Charleston, that we should leave as little as possible to chance or stress of weather.'" Here, Dahlgren tried to demonstrate that Gillmore, at the time, had requested the assistance of the Navy, and only later claimed that it had not been needed. The 7 July letter does not appear in his volume, the OR, or the ORN. Dahlgren copied a portion of it into a manuscript he sent to the historian John William Draper. The section he copied reads: "I will recapitulate the arrangements for co-operating already agreed upon by us; as follows:—1st I am to attack Morris I. on Thursday morning next, &c—[. . .]3d—The Navy is to enter the channel abreast of Morris I. early in the morning,–say about sunrise, &c—[. . .] My desire that there should be a perfect and cordial understanding between us in these combined operations &c." John William Draper Family Papers, Box 2, Library of Congress.

30 JAD: "Gen. Hunter (Gilmore's predecessor) was ready on the 8th of April to do just what Gillmore did—but avers that he could not because Du Pont would not assist—then the defences were trifling—See Hunter's letter to the President—. Gen. Hunter's letter will be seen at page 110 of the Report to Congress on 'Armored Vessels.'" Maj. Gen. David Hunter argued in his letter to Lincoln that if the Navy had operated in support of his troops on 8 April, instead of attacking the Confederate fortifications on their own, he would have realized great results. Because Du Pont had not listened to him, he alleged, the Confederates had been able to reinforce their defenses. The letter appears in *Report of the Secretary of the Navy in Relation to Armored Vessels* (Washington, DC: Government Printing Office, 1864), 110–12, as well as OR 14: 455–57.

31 Dahlgren's report on the actions of 10 and 11 July 1863 is found at ORN 14: 319–21.

"The iron-clad *New Ironsides* under sail." Engraving, c. 1885.

Library of Congress, Prints and Photographs Division, LC-DIG-ppmsca-33816.

15 Mortars—he said "the result must be a success for us"

The attack did not come off until the 18th July—the work ashore being delayed by heavy rain—On the 16th the Gen. visited me—I observed that he did not seem so sanguine and he said he depended on my vessels—

On the 17th the Gen. signaled that he was not ready—I replied that it was better not to delay, as we had all our force and the enemy could increase his I could see them at work strengthening—[32]

July 18th—heavy rain—which retards things ashore—the Gen. signals he will be ready by noon—[33]At 11½ I went on board the *Montauk*. Capt. Fairfax[34]—and led up the channel—followed by the *Patapsco Nantucket*, *Katskill*, *Weehawken* and the *Ironsides*[35]—about half an hour after noon I opened with the first gun from the water—soon the firing was general from ships and from batteries—As the tide was low the shoals kept all of us some 1200 or 1300 yards

32 Dahlgren notes this in his diary; Madeleine Vinton Dahlgren, *Memoir of John A. Dahlgren: Rear-Admiral United States Navy* (Boston: James R. Osgood and Company, 1882), 402.

33 According to his diary, Dahlgren notes that at 9:30 a.m. he received the signal that Gillmore would attack at noon. Ibid., 402.

34 Cmdr. Donald M. Fairfax had been placed in command of *Montauk* in April 1863 after her previous commander had returned "to the North in consequence of ill health." ORN 14: 131.

35 Abstracts of the log books for these ships are printed in ORN 14:363–365.

from the fort—but at 4^{OC} it had flowed sufficiently to get nearer—I ordered the anchor of the *Montauk*, up and closed steadily with Fort Wagner until less than 300 yards from it—then down anchor and continued to blaze away—the rebels left their guns and ceased to fire—As I stood outside on the top of the Turret not a head was to be seen,—some of the officers near me said,—the rebels had left the work—

About sunset, a note came from Gen. Gillmore saying he had ordered an assault,—as the light of day was fading we could [see] the masses of our soldiers coming along the beach, but lost sight of them in the darkness before they reached the fort—Presently the darkness was lighted up by the flashes of artillery and muskets—We could do nothing,—to fire, might cut down our own men by hundreds, for they were outside the rampart,—the rebels were in and sheltered—we could discern nothing but the flashes For an hour and a half the contest was maintained—Shaw and many officers and men were stricken down[36]—some of our men got in to the work and held one of its salients—if they were supported there was a chance for us—it was said they might have been and were not—of which I know nothing—At length all was hushed—the absence of all indication from the work told too well that we had it not—

It was 10^{OC} when the ironclads were hauled off and the weary crews were allowed to rest as well as they could in the sweltering heat of a southern July night it is said, and I believe authentically that our loss was 1500 men—[37]

The next morning I sent ashore the flag Lieut and Surgeon Duvall[38] under flag of truce to ask for our wounded, or if refused to offer medical aid for them—both were refused—many were lying where they fell—and were seen by our officers who landed on the beach near the fort—Of course I could not fire that day without danger to these poor fellows, so we passed a quiet Sunday—

That night it was made known to those concerned that the blockade had at last been made effective—a blockade runner contrived as usual to get through the outer vessels and was rejoicing in a clear way to the city, when her course was arrested, almost under the rebel batteries by the astounding report of a XV^{in} gun and the close passage of its huge shell—a Monitor which I had pushed up close

[36] Col. Robert Gould Shaw led the 54th Mass. Inf., an African-American unit, against Fort Wagner.

[37] Dahlgren's report on these operations, including the delays, the activities of his fleet on 19 July, and mention of Gillmore's sunset note, can be found in ORN 14:359–60. Gillmore's casualty returns give the number of killed, wounded, and missing during the 18 July attack as 1,515. OR 28, Part 1:210.

[38] Lt. Samuel W. Preston and Surgeon Marius Duvall.

to Sullivans I. had detected the steamer, and ever ready Geo. Rodgers quickly fired—alarmed and confused the evil doer lost his head, and struck on the dangerous shoal near by—of course there was a movement at once among all the vessels and even signals were seen that the Rebel ironclads were coming out—next morning disclosed the truth,—the newcomer was a wreck on the shoal, and remained till the end of the war a warning to others on like errand—[39]

Thus the blockade was perfected by the ironclads alone,—two months before our troops covered the island and while Wagner was still in rebel possession; though it is pretended that it was effected by our batteries on Morris I—rather oblivious of facts—

The day after I was much afflicted by learning that my son Ulric had been dangerously wounded near Gettysburgh[40]—while on the other hand his elder brother had the good fortune to be present at the capture of Vicksburgh and commanded a battery of IX^{in} Navy Guns (my own) landed by Adm. Porter to assist[41]—So, both of my boys are aiding as well as they can in the country's cause—There is but one more but he is a boy, and a Midshipman in the Navy—

The course of operations on Morris I. must be changed—Wagner will not be taken by assault merely—the experiment has cost too much blood—if this price were necessary to "make manifest its real and concealed elements of strength"[42] it was more than we could afford,—on the 20th July Gen. G. wrote me that he had

[39] These events took place on the night of 19–20 July 1863. Initially, Capt. Joseph F. Green, in command of *Canandaigua* had pursued the "large side-wheel steamer." The blockade runner entered the Pumpkin Hill Channel, until Green backed off in case the steamer attempted to get back outside the blockade. Dahlgren reported that after this, Cmdr. George W. Rodgers, in command of *Catskill*, had forced the steamer to ground. See reports of Dahlgren and Green, ORN 14: 374–75.

[40] Ulric's leg was wounded during fighting at Hagerstown, MD, on 6 July 1863, during the Gettysburg campaign. He returned to Washington to recover, but his foot did not heal and his leg had to be amputated. The amputated leg was buried at the Washington Navy Yard. Dahlgren, *Memoir of Ulric Dahlgren*, 168–79.

[41] Charles Dahlgren managed a pair of IX-inch guns; Adm. David Dixon Porter noted that they "were admirably served." ORN 25: 279.

[42] JAD: "Gillmore's report Sec. 82." Gillmore also wrote that "the truly formidable character of the armament of Fort Wagner, its hidden resources, and the great strength and capacity of its bomb-proof shelter, could not yet be fully developed," which, in his opinion required an attack to discover. Q. A. Gillmore, *Engineer and Artillery Operations Against the Defences of Charleston Harbor in 1863; Comprising the Descent Upon Morris Island, the Demolition of Fort Sumter, the Reduction of Forts Wagner and Gregg. With Observations on Heavy Ordnance, Fortifications, Etc.* (New York: D. Van Nostrand, 1865), 35.

"lost 33 per. cent. in killed, wounded &c" of his force—[43] Ten days after landing with scarcely the loss of a man—

It only remained to proceed to engineer the rebels out of Wagner—a tedious process—which might be sure enough as far as regarded Wagner but also gave time to the defence to make all the preparation which might be needed to establish fully other points in lieu of Wagner & Sumter—for the capture of Sumter was deemed to be involved in that of Morris I. and to depend on it—from the island, Sumter had been reduced in April 1861—

About this time I received from the Department, its acknowledgment of my No. 1[44]—in which I announced that Gen. G. had asked for assistance, and having no instructions, that I had taken the responsibility—and asked for the instructions of the Depart.—The Department in reply encloses its instructions, which it seems had been sent to Dupont but in the haste of leaving—were not turned over to me—they were dated the 6th Jun 1863, and ran thus:—

"Gen. Gillmore has been ordered to take charge of the Department of the South, and you will please afford him all the aid and assistance in your power in conducting his operations"—Signed by the Secretary of the Navy—[45]

Thus the Department confirmed to me without change in previous order to Adm. Dupont—after it was aware that the operations on Morris I. had begun What was the gist of these instructions?—the Navy was to assist Gen. Gillmore,—in doing what?—while he was "conducting his operations?"—not a word of that long plan which Gen. G. has detailed as the result of an agreement—nor had there had been a word on the subject to me from Gen. G. it was not even mentioned in the paper sent me by him in which he says "I will recapitulate the arrangements for co-operating already agreed upon between us, as follows:"—dated July 7th—and which is excluded from what he gives as the

---

[43] Gillmore further added that: "My actual loss in killed, wounded, and prisoners will not fall far short of 1,200 men; as many more are laid up by sudden sickness, occasioned by excessive fatigue duty. With this more than triple decimation of my active available command, I hesitated to incur any further immediate loss in the absence of powerful reasons to the contrary." ORN 14: 381.

[44] Dahlgren reported that he had moved immediately to assist Gillmore; "there was no time, therefore, to obtain the views of the Department on this subject." He also requested that "If the Department has any specific instructions to give upon such subjects I shall be happy to conform to them." ORN 14: 311.

[45] This was the entirety of the order; see ORN 14: 241. The Navy Department asked Du Pont in 1864 whether or not he had given a copy of the order to Dahlgren. Du Pont replied that "I do not recollect having given Admiral Dahlgren a copy of the order in question." He did aver that "I showed him the order . . . and I gave Admiral Dahlgren all the information I possessed that could be of service to him." ORN 14: 242.

correspondence between him & myself—

A survey of my means showed that they lay in the Ironclads alone—there were,—the *Ironsides*—and six Monitors available for Charleston—one Monitor at Wassaw to check & blockade the rebel ram *Savannah*—so that I had one Monitor and the *Keokuk* less than Dupont on & after the 7th April—which I only mention because one book that speaks very authoritatively says my force was greater—

As a curious instance of Gen. G. appreciation of the rebel enterprise I may mention that on the 25th July when it might be supposed that he was securely established he wrote me asking for "a strong force of Boat Howitzers abreast of his advanced line each morning for a few days"—which does not look like that independence of the naval force which was afterwards avowed—[46]

About this time I was desirous of bringing the *Pawnee*'s fine broadside of IXin guns to bear on Wagner, after the ironclads had silenced the guns, but Gen. G. objected to her removal from Stono, where he considered her essential to his position—He added "In my opinion no impression has yet been made on the strength of Fort Wagner and I doubt if the bomb-proof shelters there can be effected by any number of guns firing horizontally"

About this time I began to have some evidences that the enemy were working their torpedoes.—one just missed the *Pawnee* and destroyed her launch—[47]

In the early part of August the hot weather of this climate and the incessant labor of the men, with reduced crews began to produce their natural effects and to bear heavily on the men—

About the 11th Aug. there was much excitement got up ashore—the General signals at Two O.C. in the morning "Wagner has opened with grape and canister. An assault may be intended. Please be ready with gunboats."—(Which is not in that correspondence)[48] Though the Monitors were ordered into action at once—The Gen. followed his first telegram in half an hour with a Please—"open as soon

---

[46] Dahlgren noted Gillmore's request and ordered that "the howitzers will use canister and will be placed so as to sweep the approach to our lines." ORN 14: 396.

[47] Cmdr. George B. Balch reported that at midnight on 16 August 1863, "a torpedo exploded under the stern of the *Pawnee* . . . and totally destroyed the launch; but did not injure the ship; another torpedo went off within 30 yards of the ship at 4 a.m." ORN 14: 445.

[48] This signal does not appear in the OR or ORN. Dahlgren's staff logbook does record it as being received at 2 a.m. The entirety of the message appears above. John Adolphus Bernard Dahlgren Papers, Box 38, Library of Congress.

"Admiral Dahlgren's flag ship *Philadelphia*—Off Charleston 1863." Drawing on paper; Alfred R. Waud, 1863.

Morgan collection of Civil War drawings, Library of Congress, Prints and Photographs Division, LC-DIG-ppmsca-21376.

as possible—the enemy's fire is heavy"[49]—in short order the Monitors were at

[49] Gillmore sent this request by telegram at 2:35 a.m. Dahlgren replied: "All right." ORN 14: 436.

work clearing the whole ground between our lines & Wagner[50]—The night was still and the bugles and drums ashore were heard quite lively—The Staff-Log of the fleet has the entry "at 3:30AM Admiral Dahlgren went up the harbor to examine personally the state of affairs"[51]—it was my invariable practice to look after matters myself—and this morning coming down from the front in my barge, some of Wagners heavy shot came quite close enough to my boat[52]—such incidents I note occasionally to show how quickly the Navy was appealed to when any danger was apprehended—

And the feeling which inspired me towards the military is exemplified by a letter received from Lt. Preston—He was my Flag Lieut and being much weakened by the climate I permitted him to return North for a while[53]—and directed him when at Wash n. to see the President[54] and endeavor to explain away the impressions produced by Gillmore's injudicious unlucky assault and to suggest more men for him—It will be remembered that Preston afterwards fell at Fort Fisher,—he was one of the most gifted young men that I have met with—he wrote me,—

"The failure in the assault of the 18th has injured Gillmore very much in military circles here. From the President down I found a rather positive dissatisfaction. The general view taken of it, is that it was a rash and useless expenditure of men." Preston goes on to say that his representation had the effect of modifying their feelings,—and that the President ordered 5000 men to reinforce, tho' Gen.

50 The logs of *Catskill* and *Patapsco* give details on this action. ORN 14: 436.

51 The staff log lists the time of Gillmore's message as 2:30 a.m. Within ten minutes, *Catskill* was underway, and the monitors opened fire on Wagner at 3:10 a.m. The quotation above appears in the staff log. John A. Dahlgren Papers, Box 38, Library of Congress.

52 Dahlgren noted in his diary that on this occasion "The Wagner firing *passes repeatedly a few yards from my boat.*" *Dahlgren, Memoir of John A. Dahlgren*, 407.

53 Preston left Charleston on 30 July aboard a supply ship and returned by the start of September. He had been suffering health problems since May. Dahlgren, *Memoir of John A. Dahlgren*, 406. Du Pont mentioned that "Preston has been taken twice with fainting spells." Samuel Francis Du Pont, *Samuel Francis Du Pont: A Selection from His Civil War Letters:* Vol. 3, *The Repulse: 1863–1865*, ed. John D. Hayes (Ithaca, NY: Published for the Eleutherian Mills Historical Library by Cornell University Press, 1969), 139.

54 Gustavus Vasa Fox took Preston to see Lincoln who asked the pair why Dahlgren had not been able to take Charleston. Fox pointed out that a "purely naval attack" would not do, and impressed upon Lincoln the need to send more troops to Gillmore. Du Pont, *Civil War Letters*, 230.

Halleck was opposed[55] to it[56]

We shall see that while I was then endeavoring to do the duty of a comrade to Gen. G— he not long after had little hesitation in the use of means calculated to save himself by shifting to me the disappointed expectations of the public—

Aug. 17th—According to arrangement this day was to put to trial the labors of a month and more—the trenches had been advanced and heavy batteries erected which to were to fire over Wagner at Sumter—the work had been prosecuted steadily under cover of the Naval fire whenever it was needed—considerable bodies of troops had arrived from the North to reinforce Gen. Gillmore and great expectations were raised as to the result—Early in the morning the shore batteries began, and the Ironclads stood in to the attack—The *Weehawken* led with my flag—anchoring about 1000 yards from Wagner the other Monitors and the *Ironsides* took convenient positions and opened fire as they did so—Wagner and Gregg replied briskly firing round and grape—About 8½OC the tide favoring I caused the *Weehawken* to be shifted closer to the Fort and anchored about 450 yards from it—Fort Moultrie was also firing and making good practice. About this time the *Katskill* was seen to withdraw from the action, but I was too busy with the general business to give it much attention—At 10OC Wagner was silenced and I shifted my flag to the *Passaic* steaming with the *Patapsco* up towards Fort Sumter—these Monitors had rifled guns—as soon as we opened on Sumter the fire of Gregg and Moultrie was directed to these two vessels—as well as that of Sumter

At noon, the rebels being silenced I made signal to withdraw—it was then that I learned of the death of Capt. Geo. Rodgers—my Fleet Captain—at that time a loss almost irreparable—a heavy shot had struck the roof of the Pilot

55 On 28 July 1863, Halleck wrote Gillmore that "you were distinctly informed that you could not have any additional troops, and it was only on the understanding that none would be required that I consented to your undertaking operations on Morris Island." OR 28, Part 2:29.

56 JAD: "Preston also wrote that reinforcements would be sent—The *Richmond* with her fine battery was ordered from the Gulf—The Monitors *Lehigh*—*Sangamon* also the *Canonicus* & *Onondoga* (double turret) about 1st Octr." Welles had written Dahlgren on 28 July that the steam sloop *Richmond* would be sent to Charleston, along with several smaller steamers. On 9 October, Welles let Dahlgren know that *Canonicus, Onondaga, Sangamon*, and *Tecumseh* would join Dahlgren's squadron once work had been completed on them. ORN 14: 401; ORN 15: 26.

Officers and crew of *Catskill* with boat howitzers at Charleston Harbor. Lieutenant Commander Edward Barrett sits atop the turret in front of the pilot house. The view shows indentations from battle damage on the turret, as well as how the XV-inch Dahlgren gun could not fit through the porthole in the turret. Glass negative, 1865.

Library of Congress, Prints and Photographs Division, LC-DIG-cwpb-02977.

House, killing himself and another officer and wounding the others[57]—Towards the end of the day the Gen. telegraphed that the enemy might make a sortie in the night, would I put in the Monitors—

On the 21st of Aug. the firing from the batteries had dilapidated Sumter very effectually on the faces towards us—but the Northern faces could not be seen,

57 Rodgers and Acting Assistant Paymaster Josiah G. Woodbury had been killed when "a shot struck the top of the pilot house, fracturing the outer plate, and tearing off an irregular piece of the inside plate of about one square foot in area, and forcing out several of the bolts by which the two thicknesses are held together, pieces of which struck" the two men. Pilot Abner C. Penton received a slight wound to his scalp, while Acting Master's Mate Peter Truscott suffered a concussion. ORN 14: 458, 458–59.

and only inference was possible—So I decided to feel them that night and started in the *Weehawken* before midnight—unfortunately the leading Monitor got on a shoal and by the time I knew she was off it was too late to get into good position and do much, so I was obliged to steam down again

The attempt was renewed the next night as soon as the moon set—some delay & confusion ensued in getting into position, but this was finally accomplished and we opened fire at as near a range as the Chief Pilot considered could be attained without becoming entangled in the obstructions[58]—The delay and confusion inseparable from managing vessels in the darkness without any mark to steer by, and getting into position had delayed our beginning to fire until three O'C—so that an hour or an hour and a half would disclose our force & position to the fire of all the batteries on Sullivan's I—So we fired away as rapidly as circumstances permitted—Moultrie replied and the unusual force with which her shot told on the iron plating, was token of our being close to—As if to embarrass our aim still more a heavy fog arose and enveloped every thing, so the firing from my own vessel was performed by using a star to sight by—We did not move until broad daylight had come and it was 6½^{OC} when I signalled to retire—Battery Bee, Fort Moultrie & Beauregard were now pounding away rapidly—

Gen. Gillmore had been certain that the "offensive power" of Sumter was destroyed, but not withstanding, some shots were fired,—proving otherwise—in fact we found subsequently that many of the lower casemates were in serviceable order & heavy cannon mounted—

The next day being Sunday The weary crews of the Monitors were permitted to rest

On the 24th and 25 it blew from S.E. and, made too much sea for naval work—this wind is the worst experienced here, and the Monitors have lost too much speed by the fouling of their iron bottoms to be trusted near the narrow passage between the forts & obstructions—

The powerful barbette armament of Sumter had now been disabled and probably the guns also in the upper tier of casemates, but there was no reason to suppose that this was true as regards the lower tier of casemates on the North & N.E. faces which look directly on the passage and were farthest from our batteries—the long and powerful line of works opposite on Sullivans I. was untouched, and it was perfectly natural to suppose that the enemy had not been idle since the day of our landing (10th July) a period of six weeks in strengthening their interior

[58] These impediments included, at various times, pilings, floating booms, rope obstructions, cables, contact torpedoes, and command detonated torpedoes. Browning, *Success Is All that Was Expected*, 157–58. Depictions of some of these appear in ORN 16:390–95.

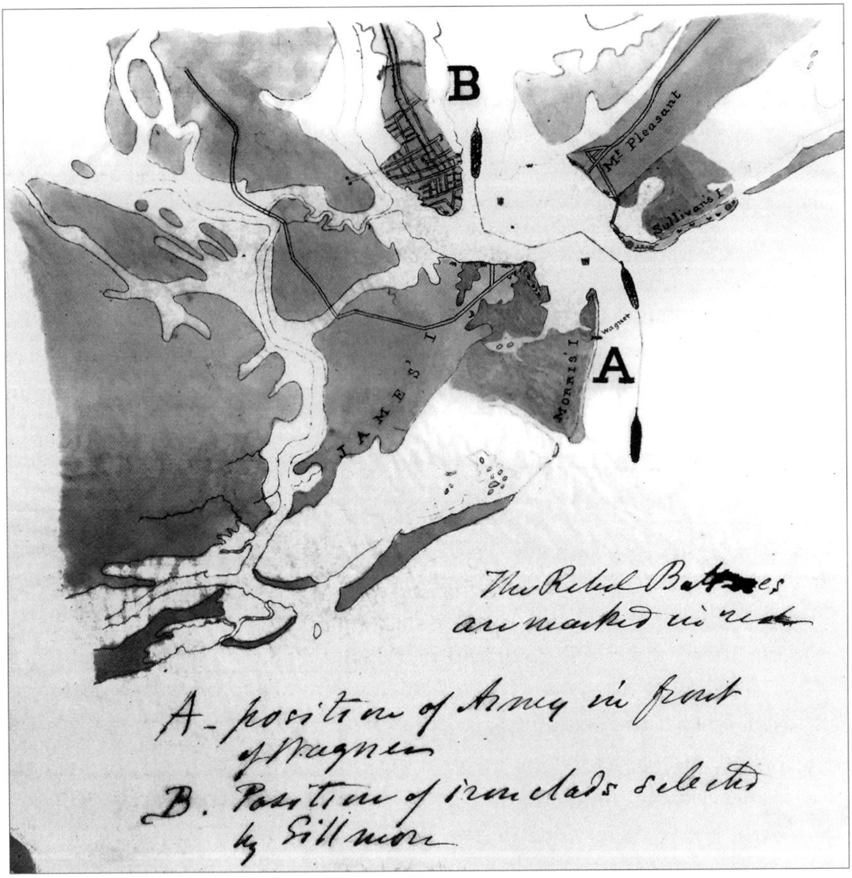

John Dahlgren drew this map after the war to show the attack of the night of 22–23 August. The square North of Morris Island shows the position of Fort Sumter, while Batteries Beauregard and Bee and Fort Moultrie are opposite on Sullivan's Island. At the top, he wrote "Channel & Course of vessels in blue—". Below the map he wrote "The Rebel Batteries are marked in red" and "A—position of Army in front of Wagner" and "B. Position of ironclads selected by Gillmore."

Library of Congress, John William Draper family papers, 1777–1951.

defences—indeed this was confirmed by what we heard and saw—especially in the huge bomb-proof that had been completed at Fort Johnson—

Still I concluded without any conference with the General to feel the defences at the entrance and be governed accordingly,—proceeding as far as their strength relatively to my means would warrant—

As already mentioned the weather allowed no fair opportunity on the 24th & 25th—and I took the 26th as the first night that was possible—though appearances were very threatening—

I went on board the *Weehawken* and about 9^{OC} the Monitors were underway—the ebb tide was so strong that it was 11^{OC} before we were abreast of Wagner—when a heavy squall of wind & rain shut the other vessels out of sight—obliged to anchor—when it cleared away, up anchor and went on—about midnight became so thick with rain that we could not see and had to anchor—About 2^{OC} Ensign Porter[59] who was in charge of the boats to remove the obstructions came to me and reported that "it was too thick and foggy and rough to do anything with the obstructions" (Log)—I was anchored about 600 yards from Moultrie, the other Monitors were in company, the rebel steamers could be seen inside patrolling the channel and the flood tide was setting like a sluice—it would have been madness to risk the Monitors amid such circumstances and I reluctantly withdrew as the Pilot declared that a S.E. gale was coming on—it was now so dark that the Monitors could hardly see each other and it was necessary to send an aid (Lieut. Forrest)[60] in a boat to give the order—The rain came down in torrents and when the anchor was up, it was for a while a question whether the *Weehawken* moved against the strong tide and wind—at last she gathered way slowly and it was not far from morning when we regained the anchorage—

Soon after I had reason to believe that Gen. Gillmore was mistaken in saying the offensive power of Sumter was destroyed—literally it might be that its guns were no longer capable of damaging the ironclads, and if Sumter were the only obstacle, it would not bar the passage—but the close reconnaissance of the passage by myself and by others showed that obstructions lay across the channel, which must be removed for the Monitors to pass, and were covered at one end by the guns of Sullivans I. and by the Sumter at the other—

Looking at the operation of our battery at Sumter it seemed demolished and promised what was not realised—it was fair to suppose that in such condition the garrison would have been compelled to abandon it entirely—but when we came to act on this conclusion we found that such was not the case—the garrison yet held it and if deprived of the use of heavy cannon could still use their muskets and light artillery so as to sweep the water of any boats that might attempt to remove the obstructions—

On the 21st Aug—Gen. Gillmore wrote me that "the barbette fire was very much impaired, and by tomorrow noon there will be nothing there to interfere with a near approach of the Monitors to that place"—the idea of passing in is

[59] Ens. Benjamin H. Porter. On 25 August 1863, Dahlgren had asked for "a few volunteers for a special service" and authorized Porter to select these men and assemble boats for the purpose of clearing obstructions. ORN 14: 514–15.

[60] Flag Lt. Moreau Forrest.

not even hinted at—only a near approach—that near approach was tried and Gen. Gillmore's batteries were never one fourth as near "that place" as were the Monitors—[61]

As the abandonment of Sumter seemed to me indispensable to any success even in passing in, and the enemy was not to be forced out of it by a mere cannonade, it only remained to await the capture of Wagner, and then they must surely leave Sumter,—this was a natural expectation,—if any one knew better it should have been Gen. Gillmore who was an Engineer—

On the 2^d^ Septr. I wrote the Navy Dep:—in speaking of the results obtained "A glance at the map, and at the means at disposal, will show that the entire advantage cannot yet be realised to ourselves, because we cannot occupy the fort. The army is unable to do it unless possession of Fort Wagner is had; nor the Navy without forcing the defences by water in the shape of obstructions &c"[62]

Not disposed to give up the attempt entirely I had repeated the feeling of the entrance on the night of the 1st Septr.—taking up the *Ironsides*,—rather large for night operations among shoals—when to ground was perhaps to remain—

It was past midnight before we could get into position and some heavy firing followed for four hours;—Sullivans I—kept it up steadily—and Sumter fired but few shot probably to avoid drawing our fire—My flag was in the *Weehawken*, and I had the misfortune to have the third fleet Captain disabled—a heavy shot struck the turret and drove inside an iron splinter which broke his leg—a great loss to me—It was nearly 7^OC^ when we regained the anchorage—[63]

This observation of the night only served to confirm my belief in the impracticability of any operation inside until the enemy had left Sumter—

About this time some question arose as to Sumter having any guns mounted—My own impressions were that such was the case—as shots were invariably fired when the Monitors were high enough to open the sea face—Gen. Gillmore seemed solicitous then to believe there were none mounted,—but since exposes some inconsistencies on the subject—for instance his own "Look-out"

---

61 Gillmore's letter, as it appears in ORN, reads "The barbette fire of Fort Sumter is very much impaired, and by to-morrow noon there will be nothing there to interfere with the near approach of the monitors to that place." In the same letter, Gillmore also mentioned that he preferred that Dahlgren employ the monitors against Fort Sumter and the inner defenses of Charleston Harbor instead of against Wagner. ORN 14: 465.

62 In the letter to Welles, Dahlgren also reported on the action of 1 September 1863. ORN 14: 531–33.

63 Lt. Cmdr. Oscar C. Badger. In his diary, Dahlgren opined after the incident that "A fatality seems to attend my staff." Dahlgren, *Memoir of John A. Dahlgren*, 412.

signalled him on Sept. 1st that "We have dismounted two guns on Sumter and impaired one this AM—But two remain"[64]

Now if Gen. Gillmore's own information was correct—five guns were mounted on Sumter that day—for our fire dismounted two—injured one and left two—these were seen by the "Lookout"—therefore must have been placed on the Gorge wall or SE face—the other faces being invisible from Morris I—or in barbette on the other faces—the case mates of the three faces that would bear on the fleet could not be seen—How then could it be known from Morris I. that there were no guns in those casemates—there were certainly five besides what may have been there—I note this to show how much Gen. G. inferred when it suited his purpose—but I was sure that there were guns on those faces, for I had been close to them and had as good proof as it was possible to have under the circumstances—that there was ample offensive power in Sumter to defend the obstructions from all attempts to remove them—

Above all, how extraordinary when the time arrived that Gen. G. deemed advantageous for entering and crushing the enemy that he permitted it to pass without even drawing it to my notice!—and yet he remembers it now—In truth there was no such a programme contemplated by the Navy Dep: or it would have been made known to me—And what is more essential; to make the movement which was indicated by Gen. G. some 18 months after the event—would have been folly or treason—for it would have exposed the fleet to the heaviest losses without a ray of hope in the way of benefit—

I am the more urgent on this point because Gen. G. is so now—It will be borne in mind that during the ten or 15 days following the pounding of Sumter our troops were in front of Wagner toiling painfully in the treacherous sand to advance the trenches, and there was no little discouragement—the rebels possessed complete control of the entrance, and if the Ironclads should be pushed past the obstructions at all hazards, what next?—along the line of shore were powerful earth batteries terminating at the City—Could the ironclads reduce them? All the efforts of Gen. Gillmore's entire force with all the efforts of the ironclads had been expended six weeks upon Wagner, and Wagner still bade defiance—What then would the ironclads alone do against the interior works, which were not only more powerful singly than Wagner but which supported

[64] JAD: "330." In his book, Gillmore renders the message "We have dismounted two guns on Sumter, and injured one, this A.M. But two remain. We are firing with great accuracy." In the afternoon, Gillmore also reported to Dahlgren that "the artillery fire on Sumter to-day more accurate and destructive than ever." Gillmore, *Engineer and Artillery Operations*, 330, 331. Also in OR 28: Part 2:77.

"Fort Wagner Captured Sept 6—1863 Charleston." Drawing on paper; Alfred R. Waud, 1863.

Morgan collection of Civil War drawings, Library of Congress, Prints and Photographs Division, LC-DIG-ppmsca-21552.

each other, and could not be attacked alone, while Wagner was isolated and had to bear the whole brunt of our attack—But Gen. G. admits that Wagner could never have been reduced by a naval force (S240)—[65]which consequently admits that none of the interior works could be so reduced for they were of like character & much stronger. If then the ironclads could not reduce these defences, what were they to do? Gen. G. says pass the defences—that is carry the Monitors some three or four miles into the Cooper or Ashley Rivers, leaving between them and his forces on Morris, all these untouched batteries—his forces struggling alone, to gain possession of a work which had resisted combined efforts of ships & troops—the supplies of Coal & Ammunition for the ironclads cut off—a voluntary division of forces likely to ensure the destruction of both,—who ever heard of such a plan?—And yet he seriously puts this forth as a means by which to achieve success!—it would be a reflection on Gen. G. common sense to suppose

65 In his book, Gillmore wrote: "It reflects no discredit upon our navy, to say that Fort Wagner, with its garrison covered as it was by a secure bomb-proof, and with facilities for keeping its supplies of men, ammunition, and guns, unimpaired, could never have been reduced by a naval force, or by any other means than those adopted, viz.: by sapping up to the ditch of the work, and then assaulting, or threatening an assault, from the advanced trenches." Gillmore, *Engineer and Artillery Operations*, 118–19.

that he was sincere in this idea—[66]

I admit that in opposing my simple opinion to that of Gen. Gillmore, both of us being present, I leave it optional to others to decide either way—But when I say that my view is entirely sustained by Gen. Sherman, it is probable that very few will care much for the opinion of Gen. Gillmore—This opinion of Gen. Sherman I will present subsequently—[67]

It will be perceived that it is not only the difference of opinion that existed between us—but that Gen. Gillmore also adroitly kept this and the programme out of view during the period that he now alledges to have been most suitable and thus deceived me—

[66] Dahlgren wrote and crossed out after this: "an idea that I first heard of when he published his book some 18 months afterward."

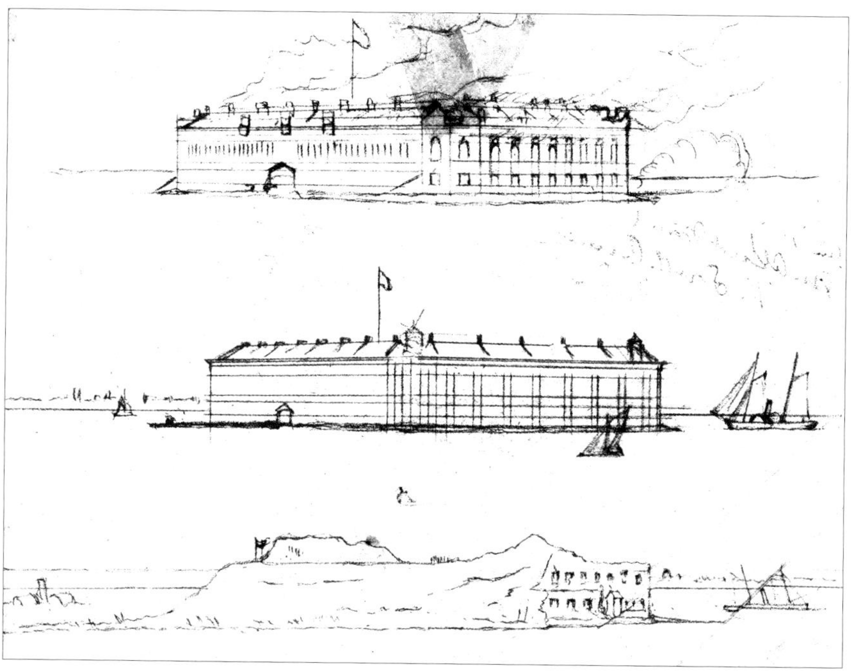

Fort Sumter. The top drawing shows the fort as it stood in 1861, the second drawing is likely a study of the elevations, and the bottom drawing shows the effects of repeated bombardments. Drawing on paper, Alfred R. Waud, c. 1865.

Morgan collection of Civil War drawings, Library of Congress, Prints and Photographs Division, LC-DIG-ppmsca-20945.

[67] See Appendix 1.

Well, the trenches advanced slowly until they were so near to Wagner on the 6th Septr—that a grand cannonade was that day opened by land & sea preparatory to an assault—this the rebels would not withstand—they had delayed the capture from the 10th of July to the 6th Septr. thus giving more than 8 weeks to improve the next line of defence—and to avoid capture withdrew

So we fell into possession of Morris I.—it could hardly be that the rebels would dream of retaining Sumter,—it looked a mass of ruin, but therein lay its strength—the rifle shot fired from batteries distant from Two to Two and a half miles had been scattered over the entire surface of the fort and thus gradually pounded the walls into dust instead of cutting a breach clear through the wall as would have been the case if concentrated on one spot—which happens when fired from a short distance—So that the operation seemed brilliant, but was deceptive—By the time we had Morris I. the fort was thus converted into a species of sand work—and the rebels having already approved the value of such a defence remained—Thus all calculations of what would happen were defeated and Gen. Gillmore found that only to a certain extent could cannon impair the offensive power of Sumter

Finding that the enemy would not evacuate Sumter—and having been well satisfied from experience that unless such were the case it would be a sacrifice of the limited force of ironclads to attempt to force the entrance unless in co-operation with the land force, I decided to attempt storming it—the difficulty of the enterprise was very apparent, but on the other hand there seemed no alternative, if anything further was to be done—So far as could be ascertained by the closest inspection which circumstance permitted the ruins of the gorge wall appeared to me to form a regular slope from the water—and Gen. Gillmore on the 23d Aug. had written—"The gorge wall is breached the entire length, the debris in several places forming a practicable ramp from the level of the water to the top of the ruins."[68] If therefore a party of sufficient force could reach the foot of this slope, they could ascend and compel the enemy to make good his defence hand to hand.

By accident I learned that Gen. G. intended to make a similar attempt and on the same night—This was elicited by a request from me for a loan of some of his boats—he answered he could not spare any as he designed to try an assault and would need them,—but proposed acting together, which of course I assented to—Owing to misunderstanding partly from signals, I sent Lieut. Preston then

[68] In his letter of 23 Aug., Gillmore averred, as well, that: "I consider the offensive power of Sumter entirely destroyed from to-day's firing." OR 28, Part 2:56

acting as Fleet Captain, ashore to Gen. Gillmore—the night advances,—no answer—I fear that there some obstacle—my own column in boats—has been advanced well up the channel so as to lose no time finally Preston comes on board—and reports the arrangement complete—and asks "may I join my division"[69]—I had been unwilling as it left me without a staff officer, except one very young—but gave way to his urgency—I said—"Are you sure all is right and no mistake with the General?" He was positive—"Very well you can go"—I never saw him again—In order to see personally to the junction of the columns and matters generally in so difficult an undertaking, my own steamer was got underway and moved up the channel when near enough, I got into a boat and pulled directly for Sumter—the log says

"At 1.30 the Admiral left the ship,—just as about to leave a very heavy volley of musketry was seen to be fired from Fort Sumter. Admiral immediately pulled for Sumter, meanwhile Fort Sumter threw up a rocket and burned a red light and almost immediately the batteries on Sullivan's and James I. opened a heavy fire."[70] On my way up the *Lehigh* suddenly loomed like a shadow in the darkness, and I paused a few moments to enquire about the boats—then resumed my course but the conflict was short—the firing of musketry about Sumter had ceased—but grenades seemed to be flying, and the shells from Fort Johnson and the rebel ironclads and Sullivan's I. were crossing in the air over the boat and screaming like mad. It was evident that our men were not in the fort—but where?—after lying on the oars for a while, pulled for then supposed position—not a sign in the darkness—then tried to find my own steamer—not to be found—the Captain had weighed anchor and steamed down, not stopping for me to return—So there was nothing but to pull for it, which we did groping as well as possible—at last by the coming down made out a vessel—and got on board[71]—I had been severely taxed—so ill for several days as hardly able to walk—had been busy all day—solicitous about the *Weehawken* battered by the rebels—and there all night in a small boat—

Events had disappointed much of my calculation—The *Weehawken* was to have lain off the beach and covered the men,—instead she got aground and compelled me to put all the other ironclads at the heavy batteries to save her—the column of Gen. Gillmore had not been seen—he says now very coolly the tide

[69] Preston commanded the third division of boats. ORN 14: 627.

[70] ORN 14: 612.

[71] Dahlgren boarded *Lodona*. ORN 14: 636.

was too low for his boats[72]—but it was fair to suppose that at midnight when Lieut. Preston left him, he would have known enough not to give assurance of assisting in the assault—

There it was however,—the assault was not only repulsed but the force of the ironclads was sadly depreciated—The *Katskill* absent under repair for new top to Pilot House, crushed in & Rodgers killed on the 17th Aug—*Weehawken* hurt below water, could not tell to what extent also leaking—had been struck below overhang while aground and bare—by falling tide—The *Passaic* reported disabled—[73]in the action of the 8th *Nantucket* at Wassau blockading rebel ironclad *Savannah*—leaving present for duty four Monitors, *Montauk*, *Patapsco*, *Nahant* and *Lehigh* with *Ironsides*—Even some of these were more or less in need of repair—The *Montauk* reported—"repairs requisite for effective service,—are extensive" (p. 246. Ar. Vess)[74] *Patapsco*'s smoke pipe "almost carried away by a shot" (p. 244)[75]

Of course all independent movement with these vessels was out of the question—if army would advance, I was bound to run any risk to assist them—but as Gen. G. did not advance,—I could only wait until he did or await the reinforcements—which it was intended I should have—

For some weeks previous to the capture of Morris I. various remarks began to appear in the Public correspondence depreciative of the Naval service in this quarter—which then were utterly incomprehensible to me, for the Gen. and myself met after and with every seeming of the best feeling which was certainly honest on my part as any one will see who will glance over the published correspondence, and note that I never spoke illy of Gen. G., but always in good terms even where there was too little reason to do so—But I believed he was what he appeared to be, and I felt that the public cause would again suffer if there were any dissensions between us—

But when the failure to assault Sumter occurred I was perfectly astonished at

---

72 Gillmore wrote that "the force assembled . . . was detained by low tide at its rendezvous in the creek west of Morris Island until after the naval attack had failed." ORN 14: 636.

73 Lt. Cmdr. Edward Simpson reported that in the ten weeks he had commanded Passaic, the monitor had been hit 90 times and that the cumulative damage had rendered the vessel disabled. *Armored Vessels*, 248–49.

74 JAD: "249 *Armored Vessels*." Lt. Cmdr. John L. Davis informed Dahlgren that *Montauk* required an overhaul of its engines, as well as extensive repairs to its hull owing to damage from enemy torpedoes and artillery fire. Ibid., 246–48.

75 Patrick Hughes, Assistant Inspector of Iron-clads, reported to Dahlgren on the damage the various monitors had received. *Patapsco* had indeed lost her smokepipe, but it had been "almost carried away by a shot from her own fifteen-inch gun." Ibid., 244.

the senseless clamor and unjust criticism that came down on me, I was blamed for making the only effort that it was possible to make if we were to proceed, whilst not a word was said of Gen. G. failure to assault with me as he had promised to do—It never occurred to the critics that to attempt to enter the harbor with only my own diminished force without driving the rebels out of Sumter, would have been to sacrifice the only sea-going ironclad squadron the U.S. possessed without any prospect of advantage—In fact there was nothing else to be done at the moment—

The land forces now set about fortifying Morris I. and there was no appearance that any other measure was in contemplation—though undoubtedly it was advisable to move against Sullivans I. and try to reduce it from the adjacent Island as we had done Morris I.

Seeing however that the purpose ashore was bent on making very sure of Morris I. I took the opportunity to have the Monitors renovated by turns, keeping no more Monitors off Charleston than were needed—Hoping that before long I could be sure of having aid from our batteries on Morris I and then with my own Monitors repaired and some new ones from the North, I could afford the loss of some vessels to get in—

Toward the end of Sept. I regretted much to learn that Gen. G. had removed his own quarters from Morris I. to the Island below (Folly I.)—it looked to me, thus removing from the immediate scene of action, as if this change of residence announced an intent to relinquish further active operations—It is true that if such were the case, it had been already disclosed to me as the purpose of Gen. G. by what he had said in my Cabin a few days previously,—that "it was absurd to expect us to advance, when together we would be weaker out of present position than the enemy"—and that "he thought it probable I would lose half the vessels in forcing a way to Charleston."—Still I presumed that these opinions had reference to the existing condition of things and that when I had been reinforced and his batteries on Morris I. were in readiness, some corresponding effort would be advisable—

But notwithstanding the entire concordance that seemed to me to exist between Gen. G. and myself,—the correspondents who were hovering about his Headquarters were not abstaining from any remarks that were calculated to depreciate my course,[76] and by inference or directly to have it understood that Gen. G. has done all that he was to do or could do and that the shortcoming was mine—At last one of them went so far as to affirm that Gen. G. and myself differed so widely that he had tendered his resignation—Before I had an opportunity to speak to Gen. G. on this subject, I received from him the following note:—

"Morris I. S.C.
Sept. 23^{d}—1863

Admiral

I am much chagrined at the reports in the newspapers about my tendering my resignation in consequence of a disagreement between you & myself—And that we did not co-operate cordially.

It is not necessary for me to assure you that I am entirely ignorant of the slightest foundation for such reports and had no idea that they existed, until they appeared in the papers. They were doubtless started by some scribling sensationist in lieu of news. I will see that they are authoritatively contradicted.

Sincerely Yours
Q. A. Gillmore

Rear Admiral Dahlgren
Present"

It will be observed that the date of this note is the 23^{d} Sept$^{r.}$ more than two weeks subsequent to the capture of Morris I.—and to the occurrence of the events which terminated our joint operations—It is also to be observed that 18 months later Gen. G. published an official report in which he[77] alledged in substance that he was in opposition to my course and that I did not in effect co-operate with him in the plan that had been decided on—

Moreover in that report he does also substantially express the very sentiment which in the note he repudiates as those of scribling sensationists—

It is certain that the statements of the note and those of the subsequent report—both subsequent to the end of our joint operations,—cannot both be

76 JAD: "In this general connection See—Dr Duvall's Journal published by the Navy Dept in the Book entitled '*Armored Vessels*' page 273—." Surgeon Marius Duvall's journal provided details on U.S. Navy operations in Charleston Harbor; he also mentioned prohibitions against providing information to newspapers and described how both Du Pont and Dahlgren had been treated in the press. Ibid., 273–79.

77 Dahlgren wrote and crossed out here "shows conclusively that."

Confederate *David*-type torpedo boat. Photograph, 1865.
Naval History and Heritage Command, Photographic Collections, 165-C-751.

true—which of them is not—

It will be seen that the sentiments expressed in the note are in accord with those I have above attributed to Gen. G. in conversation that passed—

Certainly such a note was calculated to allay any doubts that may have arisen in my mind—And matters were in this condition when the enemy made a practical exhibition of some of the means which had been in contemplation for use against us—About 10^{OC} at night of the 5th Octr. all were startled by some rapid firing in the vicinity of the *Ironsides*—On steaming up there I learned that a torpedo had been exploded under the *Ironsides* and created some sensation—the whole proceeding had been so novel in its character as to puzzle every one in regard to the nature of the machine—and but for an accident we might have remained in ignorance some time[78]

Next morning however two persons were captured from whom it was ascertained that it was one of a the torpedo boats of which some account had occasionally reached us—It was early in the morning when a poor wretch was dragged

[78] Accounts of the attack on *New Ironsides* by the Confederate torpedo boat CSS *David* can be found in ORN 15: 10–21.

before me, who evidently looked for nothing less than immediate hanging he was told that a full account of the machine was indispensable[79]—he was glad to find this would answer and described the "boat," as I found afterwards, with entire accuracy—there were four persons in it, and it was almost entirely submerged—It was only visible some 50 feet from the ship, the sentry hailed,—and the officer of the deck instantly jumped on the gangway and hailed too,—the answer was a shot from the boat that hurt him badly instantly followed by a loud explosion—a shock,—and a huge column of water, part of which deluged the engine rooms—the musketry of the ship opened rapidly but ceased when no further movement was observed—the column of water thrown up by the explosion had fallen partly in the "torpedo boat" nearly extinguishing the fires of her little engine—two of her party jumped overboard, but the pilot and engineer remained,—and finding that they escaped notice in the darkness, contrived to start the engine and to get back to Charleston[80]

The effect had been really serious on the *Ironsides*, and would have been far more so if it had occurred lower down—on her bottom.[81]

It may be supposed that the doubts of the sceptical part of our crews were pretty well removed by this evidence of the existence of torpedoes—there is always a number in every circle who pride themselves on being above apprehension from such invisible dangers and deride their existence,—and being irresponsible expand largely when there is no danger, or when held back from danger by the decision of those who are responsible—it was interesting to observe how the present experience disposed of the need of further argument—the interest in guarding against these hidden foes became general—

One thing was evident if the great massive frame of the *Ironsides* was so affected, the thin iron bottoms of the Monitors would be blown through without fail—

Soon after, while at Port Royal I was surprised one evening by the music of a full band near me,—suddenly a steamer came alongside and Gen. Gillmore came on board with some friends in the merriest mood—I only mention this to show

79 Presumably Pilot Walker Cannon; Dahlgren wrote, "I did not see" the other captured Confederate, Lt. W. T. Glassell. Dahlgren, *Memoir of John A. Dahlgren*, 417.

80 Lt. Glassell and Pilot Cannon abandoned CSS *David* after the attack and were captured by Union vessels; Assistant Engineer J. H. Tomb and Seaman James Sullivan remained on board *David*, restarted the engine, and returned to Charleston. ORN 15: 19–20.

81 Carpenter T. H. Bishop detailed the heavy damage to *New Ironsides* in the coal bunkers and hull near the engine room and recommended, "this ship ought to be docked as soon as she can possibly be spared from this harbor." ORN 15: 17–18.

the friendly relation that existed between us—and yet, My suspicions had been somewhat excited by seeing reference in some abusive correspondence to matters contained in confidential correspondence—

About the middle of October Gen. Gillmore came on board to see me, dined and remained several hours—I referred to some replies by letter that I had received from him in regard to operations and expressed my surprise at them differing so widely in their tenor from the conversations that had passed between us—

It is fairly supposable that if Gen. G. had any objections to urge to the Naval operations—any failure to carry out the alledged plan of operations he would then have explained himself fully—Instead, he disclaimed all idea of disagreement, or that there had been any but the best understanding between us—laughed and proposed to suppress the two last letters,—I replied that if he wished to have his letters back he could do so—I handed the last to him, which he tore up then and threw into the Stove—The works on Morris I. were said to be now nearly complete and ready to open—On the 22[d] Oct—I convened a Council of Officers, in compliance with the directions of the Depart[t.]—It embodied probably the best experience that was then to be had in regard to naval operations off Charleston—and include Capt. Rowan (now Rear Admiral) commanding the *Ironsides* Capt. Emmons the Chief of Staff—Capt. Ammen on my staff and formerly commanding the Monitor *Patapsco* on the 7th April, during the attack by Adm. Dupont—and the Commanders of the Seven Monitors—making Ten officers in all—[82]

The discussion & deliberation was perfectly unrestrained and the fullest expression was invited—I submitted all the official papers—the officers themselves were well acquainted with the ground and had been in many of the actions that had taken place—I took no part in the discussion, and limited my action merely to the business pending—

We sat in full sight of the harbor the forts, &—the vessels—it is to be taken for granted that if any Naval opinion was to be relied on, it was in this case

The Council decided by a vote of Six to four that "there would be extreme risk incurred without adequate results by entering the Harbor of Charleston with

[82] Dahlgren's report of 23 October to Welles and the findings of the council of officers are in ORN 15: 65–68. The attendees were Capt. Stephen Clegg Rowan, commanding *New Ironsides*; Flag Capt. George F. Emmons; Cmdr. Thomas H. Stevens, commanding *Patapsco*; Flag aide Cmdr. Daniel Ammen; Cmdr. Andrew Bryson, commanding *Lehigh*; Cmdr. Edmund R. Colhoun, commanding *Weehawken*; Lt. Cmdr. Edward Simpson, commanding *Passaic*; Lt. Cmdr. John L. Davis, commanding *Montauk*; Lt. Cmdr. Greenleaf Cilley, commanding *Catskill*; and Lt. Cmdr. John J. Cornwell, commanding *Nahant*.

the Seven Monitors the object being to penetrate to Charleston"

The majority was composed of the Senior Officers—Capts. Rowan & Emmons—Comdrs. Ammen, Stevens, Bryson & Calhoun—

The Council was equally divided as to whether the *Ironsides* should enter if the Monitors did—and her own commander, Rowan who was the best judge in such a matter, voted against her going in.

In favor of co-operating with the Army in attacking Sullivans I. the Council voted Ayes Nine—No: one

And unanimously that Forts Moultrie and Johnston could not be reduced by the present force of Iron-clads, unsupported by the Army—[83]

It is probable as already said that no better opinion of the Naval question was to be had—and it can not be rejected—It is decisive against the opinion of a Military officer, who was necessarily uninformed on the subject (See my reply to the Comm. on the Conduct of the War—published in their Report to Congress—3^d^ Volume 1865—38th Congress 2^d^ Session page 9.)[84]

The opinion of the Council as to entering the harbor, was also fully confirmed by the reply of Commo. Rodgers to the query of the Committee on Conduct of the War Febr. 3. 1864—See page 82—Second Vol. report of Com. 2^d^ Session 38th Congr 1865)—[85]

To those who may consider that these are merely the inevitable opinions of Army & Navy Officers differing from mere pride of opinion—I will offer Military testimony that will not be disputed—I mean the opinion of Lt. Gen. Sherman. It will be seen in the course of this narration that it was my pleasure to contribute all the efforts of my command to the interior movement of this great General from Savannah Northward in Geo & S.C.—and it may be well to note that Gen. Sherman has peculiar means for judging in relation to Charleston, because he had spent many years of earlier life on Sullivans I. and his keen powers of observation were familiarised with every spot of the locality—

I think therefore that every military doubt is removed by his opinion, if in

---

83 See ORN 15:67–68 for the Council of Officers.

84 For Dahlgren's testimony about this conference and operations in Charleston to the Joint Committee on the Conduct of the War, see JCCW 6, "Miscellaneous," 1–11.

85 John Rodgers, in response to the question "What is the reason that our navy does not now, or has not heretofore operated actively against the city of Charleston" testified that: "if General Gillmore on the same island, assisted by his artillery and the whole force of the monitors, in forty-eight days, could not capture Fort Wagner by them alone, it is perfectly certain that the monitors alone never can take the much stronger defences which line James's island and Sullivan's island." JCCW 5, "Heavy Ordnance," 82.

truth & sincerity any existed

I had informed Gen. Sherman of the destruction of the Monitor *Patapsco* by a torpedo in the course of measures to force the entrance by way of assisting his movement

The clear & proper view of what he deemed necessary was contained in his reply of 17th Jan—After explaining his design he says "I would prefer you should run no risk at all—&c"—"I think you will concur with me that in the anticipation of the movement of my army to the rear of the Coast, it will be unwise to subject your ships to the heavy artillery of the enemy or his sunken torpedoes"[86]

The great confidence which I knew must attach to the opinion of this distinguished officer,—his perfect knowledge of the localities about Charleston and his fearless truthfulness led me to seek his opinion on the subject as better calculated than any other to dispose of Gen. Gillmore's assumption—

Gen. Sherman replied at length and as decisively as one of his own battles—I wish I could give his whole letter—it is conclusive & explicit on every point involved and will always be to me a never failing source of satisfaction—as it entirely confirms the course which I took—He does not believe that my passing Sumter would have caused the evacuation of the Forts & city—"but that the fleet would have been subjected to a terrific fire from the circle of batteries that would have crippled every ship and rendered the fleet useless for other purposes. The enemy could well have afforded to exchange the City of Charleston for the fleet."

"To the second question I answer that of course the passage of the Ironclad fleet into the inner harbor before Gen. Gillmore had reduced battery Wagner would have been still more imprudent."—

"To the third question I answer that had you run into Inner harbor and up Cooper river the enemy could easily have held all his works on James & Sullivan's I. without trouble as the fire of your ships could not reach the road from the interior of those islands."[87]

He also observes "<u>that all</u> the attacks from the front were playing into the hands of the enemy, who of course had reason to rejoice at every attack from that quarter"—[88]

These extracts are quite sufficient to dispose of the absurd notion which Gen. G. by his own account would was willing to impose of the ironclads, but which

[86] For the full letter, in which Sherman details his plan of operations, see OR 47, Part 2:67–69.

[87] JAD: "Gen. Gillmore affirmed that if the ironclads were to run by the batteries, the rebels would abandoned these islands."

[88] See Appendix 1.

he was very far from venturing to touch himself

I am free to say that I do not believe that Gen. G. ever seriously entertained such a plan, until subsequent events made it useful to cover up his own failure to meet the expectations of others—whether tendered by him or not—

Nor do I believe that such a plan ever was entertained by the Navy Dep.—for if it had been I should have been apprised of it—which I never was—

The opinions of the Council & Commo. Rodgers—and of Gen. Sherman effectually dispose of the value of the Plan—and it is also must be plain that nothing of the kind ever was agreed upon as stated in Gen. G.s official Report

Of the conduct of Gen. G. to myself in leading me to believe by word and writing that we had been acting harmoniously, up to the date of the letter, when he was permitting other impressions to find their way into the public prints and did substantially avow them afterward I leave to the consideration of every honorable man

It should be borne in mind that all these remarks are to defend myself against the scandalous and unfounded statements of Gen. G. in his official report—that I never made any attack upon him or his conduct,—but in my desire for the public interests and to sustain a comrade I sustained and praised him to an extent that I now find it difficult to justify—

On the 25th Oct[r.] Gen. G. asked me by letter if I would "make a demonstration in his favor with the Monitors and the *Ironsides*,—in case he determined to attempt the occupation of Sumter within the next few days"—"If so I shall see you and arrange details."[89]

I replied the same day—that I would "give him all the support in my power"—and would be pleased "at any time to see him in order to arrange the details referred to."

Next day he came on board, but said not one word of that determination to occupy—but remarked that he was trying range on Sumter—I replied that I had heard of it from my own look outs and had ordered two Monitors to assist with Rifle Cannon—

The second cannonade of Sumter now began from the new land batteries—it was continued with more or less steadiness for some weeks, and was assisted by

[89] The letter is not found, but Dahlgren makes note of it in his journal. Dahlgren, *Memoir of John A. Dahlgren*, 420. In another manuscript account of the siege of Charleston, Dahlgren quoted the same portions of the letter. He added afterwards that "this unconditional reply will exemplify the manner in which I believe I never failed to meet propositions of Gen. Gillmore that concerned the public interests." John William Draper Family Papers, Box 2, Library of Congress.

the fire of the Monitors which I sent up daily for the purpose—Very frequently I went up in a gunboat to look at the work and felt at last compelled to abandon any hope that the rebels could be expelled by cannonade—It was also evident to me that the rifle cannon were quite ineffective against the massive rubbish of the fort—its brick walls had been pounded into ramparts of sand, on which the rifle shells made little penetration and exploded superficially—it was clear to me that the round shells from smooth bores would have done better work—But the bayonet was needed—the cannon would do no more than they had done.

About the middle of Novem[r.] in conversation with Gen. G—he seemed much inclined to a proposition looking to Sullivan's I.—and mentioned that he would divert attention from the project—by means of the newspaper correspondents—I did not then appreciate his aptitude that way as fully as it deserved though I came to it afterwards—and so did Gen. Butler, when Gen. G. came to serve with him—(See Gen. Butlers pamflet in relation to Chaplain Hudson)—[90]Certainly it was a new branch of the engineering art. I could not but observe that on this day Gen. G. was very nervous—said he does not sleep—did not all last night—I remembered his being troubled so before but attributed it to critical operations—He remarked to-day that he had never been easy until the Monitors rode out a gale safely,—as he was uncertain till then of his own position.—rather in contrast with some opinions subsequently made known

On a couple of days afterwards the rebs. suddenly opened fire on our battery on Cummings Point—which seemed to call up the vision of a landing by the enemy—absurd as was such an idea; Gen. G. telegraphed me—"Will you have some of your vessels move up so as to prevent an attack by boats on the sea face of the point?"—[91]accordingly I ordered the Monitors on picket & the tugs on patrol to attend to the matter—that Capt. Bryson did this zealously and kept in as close

[90] Butler had ordered Chaplain Henry N. Hudson arrested, ostensibly because Hudson had gone on leave and failed to return to the army at the appointed time. Butler, however, also went after Hudson for "certain libellous publications," as Butler termed them. He believed that Hudson had worked with Gillmore, then serving under Butler's command, to write letters published in New York papers critical of Butler's generalship. He further alleged that Hudson had gone on leave only to avoid an investigation into his authorship of the articles and ties with Gillmore. See Benjamin F. Butler, *Official Documents Relating to a "Chaplain's Campaign (Not) with General Butler," but in New York* (Lowell: Charles Hunt, 1865), 5. A thorough recounting of the affair, including Butler's investigation, pamphlet, and the pamphlet Hudson wrote in response, is: Howard C. Westwood, "Ben Butler Takes on a Chaplain," *Civil War History* Vol. 35, No. 3 (September 1989): 225–38.

[91] Gillmore's full telegram included the sentence "The enemy have opened a heavy fire on Cumming's Point" before the section quoted above, ORN 15:117. For the telegram and Dahlgren's report of this action, see ORN 15: 117–19.

as he could, is best shown by the fact that his vessel in the darkness was unable to avoid the shoal and grounded; the heavy batteries on Sullivans I. at once opened very heavily on the Monitor—to extricate her I signalled the other ironclads to interpose—and went up in the *Passaic*—getting near the *Lehigh*, I found that the *Nahant* had approached more nearly and went to her in my barge—Capt. Cornwell skilfully obtained a position whence he could pass a hawser to the *Lehigh*—I have seldom witnessed a sight of greater interest—The *Nahant* was only 100 or 150 yards from the *Lehigh* the shot & shell came in a storm from the rebel batteries, striking the two monitors or falling between them—amidst it—Dr Longshaw & two seamen[92] passed in a small boat to carry a line—three hawsers were cut[93]—one by shot and two on the sharp iron edges of the deck—The *Montauk* & *Passaic* were making fine practice at Moultrie to relieve us—But the *Lehigh* would not stir—the tide was at its height—I ordered the *Montauk* ahead of the *Nahant*—both to steam steadily, while the *Lehigh* backed—it was a moment of intense interest for if not floated she must remain there twelve hours—every eye was bent on the hawser & the *Lehigh*—suddenly she came off as if launched—and was safe—[94]

I had the satisfaction of promoting the seamen who went in the boat to be officers on the spot—under the fire of the enemy—shells & shot baptising them—

Though the Monitor had been thus risked to keep off those terrible rebel boats—Gen. G. never fired a shot from his batteries to help us. the *Lehigh* was badly hurt under water—and required great care to get her safely to Port Royal[95]

Novem. 24—so delighted to see my gallant son Ulric—who came down to visit me whilst his wound was getting well—how changed—wasted by suffering the loss of his leg—which nearly cost him his life,—his brave spirit was unquenched—I knew that he had lost his leg,—but when I realised it the pang

92 Assistant Surgeon William Longshaw Jr. carried the hawser twice, rowed by Coxswain Thomas Irving and George W. Leland. All three men were from *Lehigh*. Dahlgren had Irving and Leland advanced in rate for their service; the Secretary of the Navy informed Longshaw that he could present himself for examination to passed assistant surgeon after he had completed two years of sea service. ORN 15: 120.

93 Three sailors from *Nahant*—Frank S. Gile, William Williams, and Horatio Young—carried the hawser over once. ORN 15: 120.

94 Bryson's report on *Lehigh* is found at ORN 15: 119. Initially, he believed that "no injury has been done the ship by grounding that can be perceived." *Nahant*'s log of the episode can be found at ORN 15: 121–22.

95 *Lehigh* went to Port Royal in November to repair damages from enemy shot as well as a leak. ORN 15: 142–43.

Rear Admiral John Dahlgren standing next to a Dahlgren gun on the deck of *Pawnee* in Charleston Harbor. Glass negative, c. 1865.

Library of Congress, Prints and Photographs Division, LC-DIG-cwpb-02988.

was intense—[96]

Our batteries pummel Sumter lazily—evidently useless—

No reinforcements yet—hear that the Contractors cannot find workmen

Dec. 6th sorrowfully saw the Monitor *Weehawken* go down in a gale but a few

[96] For an account of Ulric's trip to Charleston, see Dahlgren, *Memoir of Ulric Dahlgren*, 185–203.

hundred yards from my own vessel—it was a sad loss—[97]

We were now in the winter—the duty performed is of the most trying kind—and falls with special severity on the Monitors—their decks would be some nine to 12 inches above water if it were still, but that is never the case in this open roadstead and the sea breaks or rolls constantly over,—the top of the turret alone is dry,—the crew if they mount to escape the close atmosphere between decks, cluster around the Stack for such warmth as it yields—no phase of life has less of comfort.—As the night comes,—there is duty at the front—watch and ward for the Monitor under the very batteries of the enemy—to check torpedo boats from coming out or English friends from running in the anchor is under foot, but the stream is ever ready, and the heavy cannon of the Turret—No duty has been done this war more grinding in its nature than that of the inner blockade of Charleston—none perhaps less appreciated—

So the writer proceeds—the blockade is perfect—but no reinforcements yet—

On Christmas day the rebels attempted a surprise in Stono—secretly established batteries and opened suddenly on the advance Gunboat—which however was not to be caught napping but returned the fire vigorously—

The unequal contest lasted until the veteran *Pawnee* got into position and opened her broadside of IX^{in} guns—which quickly drove the rebels from their guns that we picked up next day—[98]

A few days afterwards had a sight of some of the obstructions from above, which had been driven down by late gales—they consisted of bars of Railroad iron, each 21 feet long, linked together, and each bar floated in an immense mass of solid timber—they had drifted on the beach and were being hauled up—as many as 33 had so far been counted—

---

97 *Weehawken* went down with the loss of four officers and 27 men. Vessels nearby reported that "she was settling fast by the head" around 2:40 p.m., and then "made a heavy roll to starboard, then righted and sank immediately." ORN 15:170. Only five minutes passed between the time that *Weehawken* made her distress signal and when she sank. A court of inquiry found that open and improperly closed hatches allowed large amounts of water into the vessel. Dahlgren informed the Navy Department that "the mischief was really done by the entrance of too much water through hatches, hawse pipes, etc., before proper measures were taken." Ibid., 169.

98 The Confederate attack on *Marblehead*, Cmdr. Richard W. Meade Jr., resulted in three men killed and four wounded. The schooner *C. P. Williams*, commanded by Acting Master S. N. Freeman, and *Pawnee*, Cmdr. George B. Balch, assisted in driving off the Confederate forces. Meade praised his crew: "Their courage was so well displayed that the enemy, who had doubtless counted on disabling us, were forced to retire (without effecting their object) in confusion and ignominy." ORN 15:191. A landing party from *Pawnee* carried off two 24-pounder guns from the former Confederate position. The reports of Balch, Freeman, Meade, and others, are in ORN 15: 188–209.

In a conversation to-day with Gen. Gillmore he observed that he "never could perceive his ability to do anything if I went into the harbor, and thought it a great risk to our position to do so, which he was willing to say in writing"

CHAPTER 5

Siege of Charleston, 1864

1864

Towards the middle of January one of the newspaper correspondents informed me that Gen. Gillmore read their dispatches before sent and struck out what he chose—thus endorsing whatever abuse of me they chose to write—

I at once addressed a note to Gen. G. and asked if this was true—he answered by Telegraph denying the charge.

A few days afterwards he came on board and asserted that the charge made by the correspondent was a falsehood—The conversation was at length upon affairs generally—The Gen. said the War Dep$^{t.}$ had refused reinforcements, and he gave up the idea of doing anything further—he authorised me to say to the Navy Dep$^{t.}$ that he could do nothing if I went in, and considered it hazardous for me to go in—

Early in February Gen. G. asked me to assist him in an expedition up the St Johns—thither I went with vessels of such draft as could cross its Bar—troops and ships got as high as Jacksonville—the army landed, Gen. G. started it into the interior and then went back to Port Royal—presently the rebs. were encountered in force—a fight ensued and Gen. Seymour[1] finding the enemy largely superior, fell back—

On the 17th Febr. lost another vessel by a torpedo-boat—The *Housatonic*—not one of the converted merchant steamers but a fine new Steam ship of War; as before, the machine was close aboard, before seen—about 9^{OC} at night, and anchored outside in the open sea, on blockade—orders were given and obeyed quickly but in vain—in less than five minutes the noble ship lay on the bottom—of

[1] Brig. Gen. Truman Seymour commanded a Union expedition to Florida in early 1864. Ezra J. Warner, *Generals in Blue: Lives of the Union Commanders* (Baton Rouge: Louisiana State University Press, 1964), 433–34.

"Destruction of *Housatonic* by a rebel torpedo Feby 17—1864—Charleston." *Housatonic* fell victim not to a torpedo but to the Confederate submarine *H. L. Hunley*. Drawing on paper; Alfred R. Waud, 1864.

Morgan collection of Civil War drawings, Library of Congress, Prints and Photographs Division, LC-DIG-ppms-ca-21443.

the ocean—officers and crew floating around—[2]

These torpedoes have been much laughed at, but without reason—their operation would be damaging to any vessels, but almost certainly fatal to the thin-iron flat bottoms of the Monitors as was very conclusively shown afterwards—It is to be borne in mind that the Monitors off Charlestown were widely different from the <u>*Miantonomah*</u>—which has a wooden frame as massive as a Line of—battle ship—her lower deck almost as ample—defended from fouling by a copper bottom—double screw, which would turn her as well as drive ahead—and lastly two turret with four XV^{in} guns

The previous narration almost loses sight of the general duties of the squadron—the work at Charleston engrosses all—however I had other cares—the "beat" covered some 300 miles of Coast—from Murrill's Inlet S.C. to Mosquito inlet (Florida) including no less than 17 ports of the best description, requiring an effective blockade—the number of vessels in the squadron was seldom less than 70 and reached as high as 95 at one time—the labor needed to carry such an affair was immense & unremitting—The vessels particularly the steamers were always in want of something—the steam being always going,—the machines wore rapidly and the

[2] *Housatonic* had not been sunk by a Confederate torpedo boat, as Union officers widely believed, but by the fully submersible vessel CSS *H. L. Hunley*. Deserters had brought news of the Confederate submarine to the U.S. fleet earlier in January; after receiving news of what he called "the Diver," Dahlgren had ordered additional measures to guard his ships against attack. ORN 15: 238.

Lieutenant Samuel Preston. Glass negative,
c. 1863.

Brady Photograph Collection, National Archives, B-5983.

establishment at Port Royal for repairs was very large, though far from sufficient—The Coal consumed was excessive—Provisions & supplies of all kind—Cannon, powder shells &c. Then the health of the men wore out too—the climate was unfavorable and the sick went North—making a perpetual drain illy replaced by men sent in return who had never seen a ship—The Officers wore out too, and there was not I believe one left in command when I departed, who was there when I took command—The correspondence was enormous—and required a large clerical staff—Then I labored under the disadvantage of losing several Fleet Captains (Chiefs of Staff)—one so great that it is difficult to be understood—

The first one became sick and had to go home,—the second (Capt. Rodgers) was killed in action on the 17th Aug.—the third (Capt. Badger) suffered a broken leg in action two weeks afterwards—and the fourth (Lieut. Preston) was taken prisoner in the assault on Sumter—Thus in two months of continued Naval operations I lost four Chiefs of Staff which almost entirely deranged the particular duties belonging to them and threw much of them on me—The loss was the greater, that they were able men—were my only confidential references—upon I necessarily relied much in such heavy responsibilities—With them too I lost evidences of proceedings, that became invaluable when it was my misfortune to encounter duplicity & meanness where it was least to be expected—They had been present with me in every action—one wounded—another killed—and one "Preston" was captured—one of the finest officer I ever knew—he was indeed extraordinary—uniting the judgement of 50 with the dash and years of 25—He fell at Fort Fisher—[3]

Towards the end of February the Navy Department wrote, desiring to see me, when I could leave without detriment to the public service—

Before leaving had an interview with Gen. G—on the usual friendly and unreserved terms—never suspecting for a moment what he meditated—on this occasion he expressed the opinion that Fort Johnson was complete when we landed on Morris I. but that the batteries between it and Secessionville—Simpkins, Hascall & Cheres were established afterwards—

I turned the command over to Commodore Rowan and steamed North in the "*Harvest Moon*"—a side wheeler, just purchased[4]—On the 1st March got inside of Chesapeake Capes—and on the evening of the 2[d] March reached my Washington home—little dreaming that my beloved son Ulric was that night to close his eventful career on the banks of the Mattaponý—

The business at the Department related to the new Monitors which were designed to reinforce me at Charleston—the difficulty of obtaining mechanics had delayed their completion, and now that they were nearly ready it was desirable to divide them between the James & Mobile—where they seemed to be much more needed by the course of events than at Charleston—After concluding there, they should be sent to me off Charleston—Considering that this arrangement concluded all active operations at Charleston I asked the Depart. to relieve me, but was requested to remain—

Meanwhile a deep sorrow was gradually breaking in on me—The President in overflowing kindness—tried to break its force as much as possible—first a note then a message with hopeful news—then would have me to the Theatre with him, but I was too uneasy to go—then he came to my house himself with some hopeful rumor—but at last the certainty came and he sent for me—my first impulse was naturally to go to Fort Monroe Mr. Lincoln—at once said—"go—ask no one,—I will stand by you"—

On the 9th March I arrived there early—and the first to drift from the shore was a package of Richmond papers filled with such statements & comments of a fallen foe, as fiends only could indulge in—

---

3 Flag Lt. Preston, along with more than 280 other sailors and Marines, was killed during the 15 January 1865 attack on Fort Fisher at Wilmington, NC. Chris E. Fonvielle Jr., *The Wilmington Campaign: Last Rays of Departing Hope* (Campbell, CA: Savas Publishing Company, 1997), 258.

4 Dahlgren explained to Rowan his general duties as "I. Strict blockade of the rebel ports, not even permitting foreign vessels of war to communicate. II. Cooperation with the army. III. Active operations against the enemy when the opportunity offers to do so with success and advantage." ORN 15:345.

Major General Benjamin Franklin Butler. Glass negative, c. 1863.

Brady-Handy Photograph Collection, Library of Congress, Prints and Photographs Division, LC-DIG-cwpbh-04894.

His only purpose had been to rescue the wasting captives from Libby and other horrible dungeons—and these savages could only see in it, harm to themselves,—the papers which they affirm were found on him could only be forgeries—for the signature was mispelled—it was impossible that he should ever have misspelled his own name—and thus the lie was disclosed—[5]

My efforts were now given to the recovery of his body—and a request was forwarded by Gen. Butler to the authorities at Richmond—[6] who signified their assent—but afterwards sent word that they found his grave empty—the body had been removed—Meanwhile I was apprised that some persons of Union sentiment had set about to do so and had succeeded,—so the evidence on

[5] A cavalry raid under the command of Brig. Gen. Judson Kilpatrick and Col. Ulric Dahlgren had set out toward Richmond on 28 February 1864. Ostensibly, the raiders intended to free Union prisoners held at Libby Prison and other points in Richmond. The raid turned into a fiasco, and on the very early morning of 3 March 1864, Confederates found on Dahlgren's body orders detailing the federal plans, including a message that ordered the raiders to burn Richmond and capture the Confederate president and his cabinet. The plan also suggested that any of the Confederate leaders who attempted to escape should be shot. The incendiary nature of these orders—contrary to the accepted conduct of war—created a stir among Confederate authorities. Union officials would not confirm the authenticity of the orders; debate still continues about whether or not these orders were authentic or a forgery. For a full discussion of the raid and the Dahlgren papers, see Bruce M. Venter, *Kill Jeff Davis: The Union Raid on Richmond, 1864* (Norman: University of Oklahoma Press, 2016), 229–78.

[6] Butler notified Dahlgren on 10 March 1864 that he would send a message to the Confederate authorities via a flag of truce the following day. Lincoln later asked Butler to "notify me instantly so that I can let the afflicted know;" the President wished to convey personally the sad news to his friend. On 23 March 1864, Butler informed the Secretary of War that the Confederate authorities were unable to turn over Ulric's body. *Private and Official Correspondence of Gen. Benjamin F. Butler During the Period of the Civil War*, [ed. Jessie Ames Marshall] (Norwood, MA: Plimpton Press, 1917) Vol. 3: 504, 509, 547, and 571. Dahlgren's body was buried secretly in Oakwood Cemetery in Richmond. Shortly thereafter Unionist sympathizers recovered the body for safekeeping until after the war. Venter, *Kill Jeff Davis*, 239–40.

both sides concurred on the removal—(Let me here refer to my letter in regard to my son, published in the *Herald* and the *Army & Navy Journal*;—A Memoir has also been prepared for publication which will contain a full account of his life).[7] I send the discourse by Dr Sunderland his pastor—which outlines his career—

The middle of April had worn around—my time had been entirely taken up with efforts to regain my son's body—the Depart. wished me to return to my Squadron and orders were sent to me—

On leaving the President, I observed that he must not expect me to do more than hold on with the force I had—he replied "Oh! yes, that is all I ask"—He had on a previous occasion when I spoke indignantly of the abuse levelled at me, said "Well, you never heard me complain did you?"—speaking with much earnestness

I was never to see my kind friend again—and the last token from him a warm pressure of my hand between his—the tears came in his eyes as he spoke of my gallant son—

All these little remembrances are treasured now—of the noble Martyr himself thinking of one who then too was a martyr—

On the 2^d^ of May arrived at Port Royal—learned that Gen. Gillmore had just left—he takes a corps with him to join the army near Richmond—

I was surprised to learn from a General officer full confirmation of what the correspondent had charged Gen. G. in relation to myself—

By the 8th I reached Charleston—and relieved Commodore Rowan of his charge, which he had now held for Ten weeks—Two days afterwards I convened a Council of Officers—The *Ironsides* would soon return North—I knew that for the present there would be no reinforcements—could anything at all be done before the force was reduced by the absence of the *Ironsides*[8]—?—The decision was Seven to two even against a serious attack upon Sumter[9]

I now concluded to look to some of the stations of the blockade and visited as far as Ossabaw.

Towards the end of May, Gen. Foster arrived as Commandr. of the Military

---

7 The same letter from Dahlgren dated 24 July 1864 appeared in *The New York Herald* on 8 August 1864 and the *Army and Navy Journal* on 13 August 1864. *Memoir of Ulric Dahlgren*. In the letter, Dahlgren claimed that the papers found on Ulric's body were forgeries.

8 Gideon Welles directed *New Ironsides* to Philadelphia on 23 May. ORN 15: 439.

9 Dahlgren held a council of the ironclad captains on 10 and 12 May 1864. Present were Commo. Rowan of *New Ironsides*, Cmdr. George H. Cooper of *Sangamon*, Cmdr. Napoleon B. Harrison of *Catskill*, Lt. Cmdr. John L. Davis of *Montauk*, Lt. Cmdr. William Gibson of *Sonoma*, Lt. Cmdr. Stephen B. Luce of *Canandaigua*, and Lt. Cmdr. Edward Simpson of *Passaic*. Lt. Cmdr. Joseph M. Bradford of Dahlgren's staff also attended. The council voted 7–2 that it was not advisable to attack Sumter. ORN 15: 430–33.

Major General John G. Foster. Glass negative, c. 1865.

Library of Congress, Prints and Photographs Division, LC-DIG-cwpb-06720.

force in place of Gen. Gillmore—[10]

In the middle of June came a copy of a letter from Gen. Ripley, Com^{dg} inside—that 50 Union Officers had been sent to Charleston for confinement—the letter proceeds to state,—"These officers have been placed in my charge and will be provided with commodious quarters in a part of the city occupied by non-combatants, the majority of whom are women and children.

It is proper that you should know, however, that the portion of the city, in which they are located is, and has been for some time exposed day and night to the fire of your guns."

Very Respectf. &c
R. S. Ripley
Brig. Gen. Comd$^{dg.}$"[11]

[10] Maj. Gen. John G. Foster of New Hampshire graduated from West Point and served in the Mexican-American War. His earlier Civil War service had been with the Ninth Army Corps in North Carolina and Tennessee. Warner, *Generals in Blue*, 157.

[11] Brig. Gen. Roswell S. Ripley, a native of Ohio, attended West Point and fought in the Mexican-American War before marrying into a South Carolina family. He served in South Carolina in the first year of the war, and then fought with the Army of Northern Virginia through the Battle of Antietam, where he was wounded. After recovery, he returned to serve in South Carolina. Ezra J. Warner, *Generals in Gray: Lives of the Confederate Commanders* (Baton Rouge: Louisiana State University Press, 1959), 257. Ripley passed on the information on behalf of Maj. Gen. Samuel Jones, commanding the Department of South Carolina, Georgia, and Florida. Ripley's letter of 13 June 1864 is in ORN 15: 528. As noted above, the Confederates sought to reduce Union attacks on Charleston by using Union prisoners as human shields. Union Brig. Gen. Alexander Schimmelfennig noted, "Charleston must be considered a place 'of arms.' . . . In my opinion the endeavor of the enemy to force us to give up the bombardment should be the reason for its continuation. At the same time, as a means to force him to give up his barbarous practices, the simple fact of retaliation can be made effectual, as I have many places where his shells fall as he has in Charleston where mine fall. I also think that the United States can furnish as large a number of Confederate generals and field officers as they can procure of ours." OR 35, Part 2.

It seems incredible that any one would choose to record such an atrocity—[12] but it is so, and the *Charles. Mercury* of June 14th gave the names of our Officers and explained at length where they were located and why—[13]

Little to be done now on this coast except maintain a blockade and strike when a chance offers—The *Ironsides* has gone home,[14] the Monitors losing in speed from foulness and continued complaints of boilers suffering from foulness—the military force too is much reduced—

The *Manhattan* (Monitor) touched on her way to Adm Farragut—

Forwarded to the Committee on the Conduct of the War my reply to their query upon Operations about Charleston (which please see in their Report)[15]

The monotony of blockade was varied by an expedition to Stono, proposed by Gen. Foster—this was in the right direction—We entered the river on the 2d June.[16] I had two Monitors *Montauk* & *Lehigh* with the *Pawnee*, the *Donough* &c[17]—the stream too narrow for more or heavier vessels—(details will be found in the official reports)[18] I think that on this occasion we were nearer Charleston than ever before—If Gen. Foster had had more men, the results would have been important but they mustered heavily on his left wing—Schimmelfennig on the right did good work—In his quiet but vigorous way he pushed the rebels out of their lines and well back on the heavy works that commanded the river and the ground before him—and while they were thus occupied he struck boldly at Johnston far away on his right and must have taken it, but for the misconduct of

---

12 Dahlgren wrote at the time that "I am also of the opinion that General Jones and General Ripley will be fully entitled to be hanged, if they are taken, for being guilty of the intent and threat to murder . . . We should not be bragged nor bullied out of any success in crushing the rebellion." ORN 15: 530.

13 The article named the Union officers involved, including five generals and 11 colonels. The editors noted that "for some time past it has been known that a batch of Yankee prisoners, comprising the highest now in our hands, were soon to be brought hither to share the pleasures of the bombardment." *The Mercury* (Charleston, SC), 14 June 1864, 1.

14 Following Welles's direction of 23 May, Dahlgren ordered *New Ironsides* to Philadelphia on 8 June, and she departed Port Royal on 16 June. ORN 15: 512, 526.

15 Dahlgren's response to the Joint Committee on the Conduct of the War was dated 20 June 1864. See JCCW 6, "Miscellaneous," 1–11.

16 Dahlgren wrote "June" here instead of "July;" these events took place starting on 2 July 1864.

17 *Lehigh* and *Montauk* crossed at the Stono Bar, along with *Pawnee, McDonough*, and *Racer. Dai Ching, Wamsutta*, and *Geranium* covered the Edisto River. ORN 15: 555.

18 The reports are found at ORN 15: 551–58.

some of the officers—such a result would have been brilliant[19]

The central stronghold of the enemy was Battery Pringle a heavy work, well armed—the shallowness of the river made it difficult to push the Monitors nearer than 2800 yards, without grounding—The *Montauk* & *Lehigh* did excellent service and the smooth bore XI inch gun of the former, well vindicated its superiority over the 8^in^ Parrott Rifle of the *Lehigh*—it was a fair sample of competitive practice and I believe decided opinion clearly in favor of the XI^in^ so far as the experienced officers were concerned—[20]

The service of the vessel was well appreciated ashore—Gen. S. wrote me on the 6th from the right—"I take pleasure in informing you of the excellent practice by your gunboats and Monitors in Stono river yesterday."

"They drove the enemy out of his rifle pits and prevented him from erecting an earthwork which he had commenced"—[21]

On my left, I heard as follows:—

"Brig. Gen. Saxton requests me to tell you that your fire on battery Pringle is of great service to him and he desires a continuance of the same."

On the 9th the Commd General decided to withdraw the troops, as the enemy were too much in force on his left—

Next day the embarkation began and was completed in the afternoon—My steamers remained until next day—to check any movement of the enemy, then got underway leisurely—and proceeded down the river in precise line—

Received news of the *Alabama*, sunk by the *Kearsarge*—marking unmistakably the superiority of my XI inch guns—pitted against the English rifle cannon and 68pdr.—they had bragged long on these two, and had run down the XI^in^—a fair fight settled the question fully—[22]

On repairing to Port Royal found there the Monitor *Tecumseh*—Capt. Craven bound to Mobile—where a month later this gallant officer ended his

19 In his report, Foster mentioned that Col. William Gurney had been delayed in assaulting Fort Johnson, and as a "consequence . . . some of the boats got aground" and that Gurney did not use his reserve to support the Union troops that had captured Fort Simkins. As a result, the Confederates recaptured Simkins and preserved Fort Johnson. See OR 35, Part 1. Brig. Gen. Alexander Schimmelfennig, a Prussian officer who had emigrated to the United States, commanded a district in the Union Department of the South. Warner, *Generals in Blue*, 423–24.

20 Dahlgren's message on the relative effectiveness of the different types of naval ordnance can be found in ORN 15: 557–58.

21 Schimmelfennig's letter to Dahlgren of 6 July 1864 is found at ORN 15: 557.

22 Dahlgren perhaps overestimated the efficacy of his guns here; *Kearsarge* went into battle with chains providing armor for the sides while *Alabama* had no such advantage.

career—we had been friends and comrades from boyhood—[23]

Aug. 3[d]—In Charleston roads—The enemy sent out the 50 Union officers whom they had had under fire—having been forced to it, by putting 50 officers of like rank, of their own, under their fire—I received our officers on board of my own steamer the "*Harvest Moon*" Gen. Foster, Gen. Sickles & Gov. Hahn[24] of Louisiana on board and were present also I had our vessels dressed with flags and ordered the *Pawnee* to salute as the Fifty passed them—just as their steame[r] was near to mine they broke out in hearty cheers for the General and myself—then they rushed on board and much shaking of hands—The steamer *Admiral*[25] took them on board for home,—there was a fine collation for them—and we had a happy time—[26]

I had received a photographic copy of the paper said to have been found on my son—it is a base forgery—the name mispelled in the signature—Dalhgren when it should have been Dahlgren—I wrote a fitting reply to the slander,—it was published in *Herald* of 8th August.[27]

---

23 *Tecumseh*, commanded by Cmdr. Tunis A. Craven, arrived at Port Royal for repairs and coal on 8 July 1864. ORN 15: 565. During the Battle of Mobile Bay on 5 August 1864, the ship struck a torpedo and sank with the loss of most of the crew, including Craven.

24 Maj. Gen. Daniel Sickles had been severely wounded at Gettysburg. After he recovered, Sickles embarked on a tour of conditions in the occupied South. Michael Hahn was the governor of Union-controlled Louisiana. Warner, *Generals in Blue*, 446–47.

25 Acting Volunteer Lt. William B. Eaton commanded *Admiral*, a screw auxiliary. Paul H. Silverstone, *Civil War Navies* 1855–1883 (Annapolis, MD: Naval Institute Press, 2001), 81; ORN 15: 637.

26 As Schimmelfennig had suggested earlier, Union generals placed Confederate prisoners in a like situation, prompting the prisoner exchange. A list of 51 Confederate prisoners sent to Charleston is found in OR 35, Part 2. Foster reported the exchange of these 51 officers for the Union prisoners; OR 35, Part 2.

27 JAD: "also in the *Army & Navy Journal* of Aug. 13th." Dahlgren's letter appeared in the 8 August 1864 issue of *The New York Herald*. In it, Dahlgren maintained that the copy of the documents he received demonstrated "that this document is a forgery—a barefaced, atrocious forgery—so palpable that the wickedness of the act is only equaled by the recklessness with which it has been perpetrated and adhered to." Dahlgren also included sections of letters that attested to the character of his son, as well as Edwin Stanton's praise for Ulric transmitted along with his commission as colonel. The paper announced the piece with the notice that remarked on Ulric's "chivalrous character" and bemoaned that "It has remained for the father, Admiral Dahlgren, to trace the cowardly forgery to its source, and proclaim it to the world." *New York Herald*, 8 August 1864, 1, 4.

Major General William T. Sherman. Print, E. G. Middleton & Co., Cincinnati, c. 1865.
Library of Congress, Prints and Photographs Division, LC-USZ62-101486.

By the middle of Aug. we have news of Farraguts Victory in Mobile—[28]

Soon after the *Wabash* was withdrawn from the squadron—to join that preparing to attack Fort Fisher—I am losing my ten vessels of force rapidly—[29]

In October among escaping prisoners were some from the wretched pens established South—Andersonville &c one who had been in several from

[28] On 5 August 1864, Rear Adm. David Glasgow Farragut led a Union squadron into Mobile Bay. As mentioned earlier, during the action the monitor *Tecumseh* struck a mine and sank with heavy casualties. After this incident, Farragut ordered his flagship, *Hartford*, to take the lead, reportedly proclaiming "Damn the torpedoes!" Once in Mobile Bay, the Union squadron engaged and defeated the ironclad CSS *Tennessee*.

[29] Welles ordered *Wabash* to Hampton Roads on 22 September 1864. *Wabash* would later serve with the squadron attacking Fort Fisher, at Wilmington, NC. ORN 15: 684.

Belle-isle—[30]

Time occupied with the blockade and in keeping our vessels from breaking down entirely

Toward the end of Novem^{r} Gen. Foster agreed upon a movement by way of diversion—for Gen. Sherman who was now known to have cut loose from Atlanta, and looking toward the coast—

I determined on organising a Fleet Brigade—collected the men—composed it of three battallions—One of Howitzers—One of sea-infantry and One of Marines—numbers not great—not exceeding 500 men—but it was very complete & won honor—I went ashore to direct the drill myself—never considered the practice of the Navy right they will mass the pieces as in the army whereas the Navy Howitzers when landed, I always designed to be used in skirmishing order—just as riflemen are scattered[31]

On the 29th Novem the expedition moved—I took a squadron of light draft war steamers and the Fleet Brigade Gen. Foster took 7000 men—

(The operation is fully described in my official Report—to be found in the Annual report of the Navy Depart dated 4th Dec. 1865 page 215)[32]

We landed at Boyd's Neck in a branch of Broad River—After effecting a landing the Gen. advanced towards the Railroad by way of Grahamsville—the rebels entrenched the road,—our men assaulted and were repulsed with severe loss—

Gen. Foster then concluded by a rapid movement to try the Railroad at another point—So on the 6th Dec. we made a feint towards the Coosawhatchie—quickly turned up the Tullifinney[33] and landed—

(Refer again to my statements in Navy Dep^{t} Annual Report—217—&c)

Here some sharp fighting ensued in which the Fleet Brigade was distinguished—and we were able to push the rebels back on the Railroad and fortify

[30] The Confederate prison at Andersonville, GA, was notorious for its poor conditions. Belle Island, in Richmond, VA, was another Confederate prison camp. Dahlgren noted in his diary that soldiers had escaped as they were transferred from Andersonville to Charleston, SC. Prisoners made their way to the Union squadron on 6, 8, and 11 October. Madeleine Vinton Dahlgren, *Memoir of John A. Dahlgren: Rear-Admiral United States Navy* (Boston: James R. Osgood and Company, 1882), 474.

[31] Cmdr. George H. Preble commanded the Fleet Brigade, which consisted of 30 officers and 463 men. Summaries of its activities, strength, and casualties can be found in ORN 16: 104–11.

[32] *Report of the Secretary of the Navy, with an Appendix Containing Reports from Officers* ([Washington, DC: Government Printing Office] 1865), 215–17. The same report can also be at ORN 16: 72–74.

[33] The Tulifinny River.

position some 1300 yds distant—

On the 12th I had news from Gen. Sherman—was sitting conversing with Gen. Foster, when one of my tugs arrived from his army with Captain Duncan,[34] a Sergeant and a private of the Illinois Cavalry—Capt. Duncan handed me a note from Gen. Howard[35] Commdg Shermans advance—which was now near Savannah—It said "We have met with perfect success thus far. Troops in fine spirits and nearby—

Dispositions were made at once for this new state of things (See Annual Report of Depart pages 220 &c)

I had the pleasure to meet Gen Sherman on the 14th in Wassaw sound—He had brushed McAllister out of his way, and they completed the communication with my Fleet—It was agreed that Gen Sherman and myself should return to Ossabaw so he became my guest and we steamed out—It was dark when we reached Ossabaw—dinner followed and we talked over the whole subject—then we retired and had hardly settled down in the beds, when Gen. Howard was announced—Gen Osterhaus[36] was with him—I turned out and Gen. Sherman hearing the voices came out too and a general talk followed till quite late—

Next day I went ashore with the Gen. and took a survey of Fort McAllister—the rebel garrison was still there, cooking &c as if nothing had happened—Then I pulled up to the Rice mills and here the Gen. and myself parted for a while—He took horse and I went back down the river

The rebels had buried large shells about the fort—some of which burst and killed some of our men after the capitulation—which naturally exasperated Gen. Sherman—

Savannah was now the object—I went round into the Vernon river on the 19th Dec to arrange for an attack on the works there in connection with Gen. S. move—The evening brought himself,—in a small steamer tug—only an orderly with him—he thought of pushing Foster forward at the Tullifinney—while I demonstrated on Fort Beaulieu—and himself clasped Savannah—So the Gen. remained with me and we started for Port Royal—We got there before daylight and spent most of the day in arranging the various moves then Gen. Sherman & myself returned to my steamer and we started for Ossabaw outside found a

34 Capt. William Duncan, of Company K of the 15th Illinois Cav. Regt. The other men were Sgt. Myron J. Emmick (or Amick) and George W. Quimby. They arrived on the tug *Dandelion*. ORN 16: 127

35 Maj. Gen. Oliver Otis Howard led one of the wings of Sherman's army.

36 German-born Maj. Gen. Peter Joseph Osterhaus. Warner, *Generals in Blue*, 352–53.

gale—had to put into Tybee and take the inside passage—

The steamer grounded—would not float so I got into my Barge—with the General and we pulled for Ossabaw Sound—had nearly reached it when a little tug came along—looked like news—puffing under the fullest head of steam—

The Capt. held up a very small slip of paper, but it had big news—it was from our lines and announced that the enemy would not await even Sherman's rapid strides—they had scampered out of Savannah and left it to us

(All fully told in my dispatches Report of Depart Dec. 1865. page 222)[37]

Tattnall too had blown up his Ironclads

On the 23d Decem had the pleasure of entering Savannah—full of our soldiers—lunched with the General and then drove round the city,—very pretty it is

The obstructions in the river are so effectual that it will be difficult to remove them at all—

In a few days came a scare from Charleston—the rebel ironclads were certainly coming out—So I was obliged to turn my attention that way,—it might be that instead of destroying their Ironclads at Charleston as they had done the *Merrimac* and the *Savannah*, they might choose the chances of battle and the certainty of some credit—The *Ironsides* had gone North long ago, and I had withdrawn some of the Monitors to assist in operations about Savannah—They had at least four ironclads—So I picked up the Monitors near Savannah and went with them to Charleston—No attempt was made however and thus ended the year 1864.

37 *Report of the Secretary of the Navy* (1865), 222.

CHAPTER 6

The Capture of Charleston and End of the War, 1865

1865

The first day of the year found me in Port Royal—where we had news of the first attack on Fort Fisher—next day I reached Savannah and met Gen. Sherman at his Headquarters

His plans for the move are all decided and he explained them to me—the right wing to be transported to Beaufort—to move from there,—the left directly from Savannah

Next day, went down St Augustine's Creek to look at the embarcation and see that my vessels were there to assist—met the General there—rare sight—the narrow winding river.—the low but bluff banks—crowded by 20, or 30,000 men—all gazing earnestly at the vessels and the scene—I could not help remarking to the General the perfect silence that prevailed—not a sound was to be heard—I said, "they seem to have no tongues"—the Gen. smiled & replied they could make noise enough when they chose—

Such steamers as I can collect and The Army transports very busy arranging transportation of troops round to Beaufort—30,000 men not to be moved in a day—

In the middle of January had the sad satisfaction of seeing Mr Michel Hogan—who acted as guide to my gallant son in his expedition to Richmond—He had been imprisoned ever since,—had escaped three times, was retaken twice, at last got off though tracked by bloodhounds—It was Hogan who swam back over the Mattapony̆, when he saw my son left there entirely alone, standing on his crutches, and under the rebel fire—

I now returned to Charleston—convened the Ironclad Captains and apprised them that Gen. Sherman would soon move and that the fleet must prepare to assist as much as possible—my views were defined by a Confidential order—

The removal of the obstructions to begin that night—Wearied with a day's hard work—I had dropped asleep on the Sofa about bed time—suddenly was aroused—the Commander of the Monitor *Patapsco* stood before me—he briefly announced the loss of his vessel by a torpedo—it was the work of a moment—a low, dull explosion, a shock, and the Monitor settled so quickly as to be under water in <u>one</u> minute—one man below was saved he saw much in the fleeting moment allowing him to dart along the lower deck,—he happened to have his eyes directed to the Ward-Room—many officers were gathered about the table—one was seated upon it—instantly the deck was blown open—the table & all about it dashed violently upward against the deck above that formed the ceiling of the apartment,—the lights were extinguished—he heard the men desperately striving to get up the hatch—vainly—he entered the engine room—made for the hatch—<u>there</u>, free—the sea was pounding over it—some one following was engulphed by these torrent of water,—he just freed himself gained the deck—floated and was picked by some boats—In this event was pictured the fate of most of the Monitors if I had attempted to force the passage—with not even the calmness of the night, but under a storm of artillery—

I immediately got into my barge and pulled to the front—it was midnight—not a sound was audible—quiet as death—it served little purpose to row over & arrived the spot the tale had been told—

In this instance no precaution had been omitted,—there were boats on each bow, and little steam tugs—carefully feeling ahead for these wretched contrivances—but in vain—

Next day—the spot was marked by the end of the tall pipe peeping above the blue water—beneath how many brave men were silent!—[1]

This incident clearly illustrated what might have been expected in event of forcing an entrance—one two or three Monitors might be destroyed in this way, or entangled in the floating ropes—leaving only the part of an insufficient force to engage batteries to which Wagner was insignificant—

Gen. Sherman was now about to commence that splendid movement which was to carry his army through both the Carolinas—and prostrate the last hopes of the rebellion,—it was to be the final and greatest act of a career undimmed

[1] *Patapsco* sank around 8 p.m. on 15 January 1865 after hitting a torpedo. Sixty-two officers and men went down with the ship; 43 survived. The tragedy occurred even though precautions against such dangers had been taken. Dahlgren wrote, "The *Patapsco* had her torpedo fenders and netting stretched as usual around her" and "three boats with drags had preceded her, searching to some depth the water they had passed over, while the steam tugs and several boats were in different positions on the bow beam and quarter." ORN 16: 173, 174.

in brilliancy—

On the 17th Jan. he wrote me, saying—"You will have heard that we took Pocatoligo on the 15th according to my plans,—and we now have the 17th Corps Gen. Blair strongly entrenched on the Railroad. I would by this time also have had my left wing at Sisters ferry, but have been and am still delayed by the non arrival of our Stores necessary to fill our wagons. I will get all the Army in motion.—I would prefer you should run no risk at all. When we are known to be in rear of Charleston, about Branchville and Orangeburgh, it will be well to watch if the enemy lets go of Charleston, in which case Foster will occupy it, otherwise the feint should be about Bulls Bay—I think you will concur with me that in anticipation of the movement of my army to the rear of the Coast it will be unwise to subject your ships to the heavy artillery of the enemy, or his sunken torpedoes."[2]

A week later the General was gathering up for the great swoop, and I was busy making arrangements to contribute whatever co-operation my force was capable of—On the 23d we met at Hilton Head for a few hours and he then returned to his Headqrs. in the field—On the 24th he wrote me

"Dear Admiral,

Weather is now fine and promises us dry land. I will go to-day to Pocataligo and Coosawhatchie,—tomorrow will demonstrate on Salkatchie and would be obliged if you would [go] up Edisto or Stono just to make the enemy uneasy on that flank and to develope if he intends to hold fast to Charleston and Columbia both. It will take five days for Slocum to get out of the savannas of Savannah, and during that time I will keep Howard seemingly moving direct on Charleston though with no purpose of going beyond the Salkatchie—

Yours

W. T. Sherman

Maj. Gen."[3]

A few days he wrote me that Gen. Slocum had got off from Sisters ferry on the 25th[4]

Meanwhile I was occupied in placing suitable forces in Edisto and Stono

---

[2] Dahlgren omitted the six sentences of this letter, in which Sherman requested that Dahlgren forward a letter to Adm. Porter and also discussed the situation at Fort Fisher. See ORN 16: 180–81.

[3] In ORN 16: 187–88.

[4] Sherman's letter of 27 January 1865 is in ORN 16: 203.

looking to the measures that might meet the views of Gen. Sherman—On the 26th in Stono myself then went to the South Edisto and from there to Port Royal—

On the 27th—to co-operate with Foster in the North Edisto, sent the *Pawnee* there, and in the evening came the tidings that the "*Dai Ching*"—had grounded under fire of a rebel battery in the Cumbahee and after a gallant defence, destroyed [it]

—Gen. Howard with Shermans advance was moving to cross this river and had requested naval diversion—the "*Dai Ching*" was ordered—she was a purchase,—had been built for the Chinese—commanded by Capt Chaplin—threading the river under steam, he came suddenly on a strong battery which opened on his vessel—he turned, narrow as the river was & had almost got clear when the black pilot becoming frightened at the sound of the passing shot ran below—the vessel grounded,—tide falling and Chaplin finding he could not save his ship cast loose his guns and began a vigorous return—after a stout defence of several hours the *Dai Ching* being dismantled and nearly a wreck, Chaplin set fire to what was left and brought nearly every man of his crew—It was late in the evening when he entered my Cabin and announced the disaster—there was nothing to say when the defence had been so gallant—

On the 28th I examined the S. Edisto myself—And from there to Port Royal—some of the ships from Porter's fleet had joined me and required new guns instead of the rifle cannon—they had burst at Fort Fisher—I found the strongest feeling against any more of the same kind—they mounted my own IXin and XIin guns instead

The events at Fort Fisher have pretty much settled the rifle question and the naval mind is coming to its right conclusions on the subject

Feb 1st nothing from Sherman—but "<u>he is marching on</u>" we know—

Little from my son Charley—he landed with the detachment from his vessel at Fort Fisher,—his Captain was wounded and the charge of the detachment fell on him—he wrote "I fired my rifle 34 times from a rest and you know father I never miss"—I did know that his hand was steady & his eye quick He had served in the Vally down to Vicksburgh—had charge there of a Naval Battery, IXinch guns—did the good work which they are capable of—had a narrow escape from a bullet through his hat—kept up till the town was captured fell sick of the fever and barely reached home with life—

On the 4th Febr. I was in the N. Edisto found there the *Pawnee* & *Sonoma* had been pounding the batteries and actively assisting our troops sent there to harrass the rebs—Next day in the Stono—and learned then Gen. Sherman had secured the passage of the Cumbahee, but his left had not yet joined him—

"Landing of General Potter's and Admiral Dahlgren's Troops at Bull's Bay, South Carolina." Engraving, 1865.

Naval History and Heritage Command, Photographic Collections, NH59175.

On the 6th a heavy N. Easter set in with rain and continued the next day,—will be bad for our army if yet on the low grounds—

On the 8th went round by way of the Coosaw to St Helena sound to see what the gunboats had been able to do in approaching the wreck of the *Dai-Ching* in the Cumbahee—On the 10th sent two Monitors into the Stono to give weight to our operations there—and ordered three heavy steamers to Bull's Bay—In the evening I steamed into the N. Edisto—and next day into the Stono—Here the move was being pushed in a manner so vigorous by that excellent officer Gen. Schimmelfennig as to alarm the enemy considerably—The *Lehigh Wissahiccon* and a Mortar assisting by a flank fire—while the *McDonough* and a Mortar Schr. were delivering an effective fire from Folly River upon the rebels—the whole affair was very spirit & the enemy were hurrying up reinforcements—I steamed up to the *Lehigh* in the advance and gave further directions—

Soon after a dispatch from Gen. Foster announced to me that he had received a leave of absence and that Gen. Gillmore had arrived with instructions to "relieve him temporarily of the command"

It was unpleasant to be thrown thus into contact with a person for whom I had so little reason to think well of, especially as active operations required close co-operation,—however I determined that the public service should not suffer on that account—Following quickly Gen. Gillmore was announced as alongside of my Flagship—Every ceremonial which his rank demanded was observed,—and I stood on the quarter Deck to receive him—But when he tendered me his hand, I declined

A conference followed in my Cabin at which Gen. Potter[5] was also present, and the necessary measures were arranged to execute the demonstration at Bulls Bay which Gen. Sherman desired—I collected a number of my best vessels to give effect and in the evening left for Bulls Bay myself—It was a splendid night—Moon full, water smooth and a gentle breeze—About One in the morning off Bulls Bay among the squadron which I had concentrated—Among them the *Ticonderoga, Tuscarora Pawnee, Shenandoah* and a number other Gunboats—The transports with troops came along just before daylight—To Capt. Balch I assigned the charge of the vessels inside, and to Capt Stanley[6] the boats and seamen to cover the landing Gen. Potter commanded the troops—While thus engaged an aid from Gen. Gillmore arrived bringing me a dispatch from Gen. Sherman—in cipher—It was dated the 7th five days ago[7]—at the Headqrs. on the Railroad at Midway—and stated that the weather was bad and the country full of water—which might force him to turn against Charleston—the Gen. thought Charleston would be abandoned lest the garrison would be captured as well as the guns

On the 15th Febr. I was in Charleston Roads and the next day at Bulls Bay, looking after operations—the troops and vessels were working hard to make ground against the enemy—In the evening steamed down to Stono; in passing Charleston observed two large fires—they denoted the preliminary moves for evacuating—though when was doubtful—

The end was now approaching Feb. 17—Friday—In Stono—In the after the indefatigable Schimmelfennig came on board,—feeble from disease that was to prove mortal[8] he would not leave his duty while able to move—he was sure the rebels were about to evacuate—wished to feel them strongly to-night on James I. and asked me for aid,—I ordered the vessels in the Stono to cover his left flank and the *McDonough* his right from the Folly Branch—I also sent up an

---

5 Brig. Gen. Edward E. Potter served most of the war with Foster. Ezra J. Warner, *Generals in Blue: Lives of the Union Commanders* (Baton Rouge: Louisiana State University Press, 1964), 380–81.

6 Cmdr. Fabius Stanly. His report on the expedition to Bull's Bay is in ORN 16: 239–40.

7 The dispatch is printed in JCCW 7, "Sherman," 332.

8 Schimmelfennig had tuberculosis.

Aid to the Comm^{d} officer off Charleston to open the Naval Battery on Morris I. and to feel the enemy with the advanced Monitors—During the night the heavy booming of the Navy Guns I heard distinctly—loud & frequent—Febr. 18th Saturday—In the morning comes a telegram to me from Capt Scott in the Charleston Roads—saying—

"The advance picket Monitor just reports that there are no indications of the presence of the enemy on Sullivan's Island except a flag,—thinks it evacuated."[9]

Soon after heard that James I. was being abandoned—I steamed round at once to Charleston—crossed the Bar and passed up the Roads—the Captains coming on board as I passed—the mate of a captured blockade runner was now put in requisition to pilot in clear of obstructions and torpedoes—he steers close to the heavy batteries on Sullivans I.—now deserted—then we turn sharp and face "Johnson" and so passing one battery after another arrive off the city—in a few minutes I land,—all the Captains are with me—the streets are silent—the houses shut—only a few men tugging at a fire engine—for some of the rebels had left the torch behind to do its work, and make us responsible for the work,—but we were too quick,—and the fires were put out—We walked over no ashes, and all we saw were alive—no one was buried under the ruins.

Their ironclad squadron was however destroyed—Three blown up & sunk two burned on the ways—and one just ready for sea bilged—[10]

Next day I listened to the painful story of Lieut. Bradford—He was one of my officers—was wounded mortally and taken in the assault on Fort Sumter died in a Charleston Hospital—was buried by a kind friend in the Magnolia Cemetery—when known caused great excitement in the city—the body was disinterred and turned over to the Potter's field—the dust of the Union soldier was not worthy to lie with the best of Charleston!—I took the steps required to do

---

9 Dahlgren received Capt. Gustavus H. Scott's message at 10:45 a.m. ORN 16: 370.

10 The Confederates destroyed the ironclads CSS *Charleston,* CSS *Chicora,* and CSS *Palmetto State.* The ships on the ways have not been identified; the ship bilged was CSS *Columbia*, which had run aground near Fort Moultrie. Union forces also captured the steamers CSS *Lady Davis*, CSS *Mab*, and CSS *Transport.* J. Thomas Scharf, *History of the Confederate States Navy from Its Organization to the Surrender of Its Last Vessel,* 2nd ed. (Albany: Joseph McDonough, 1894), 706.

him & his cause justice—[11]

Meanwhile to give the enemy no breathing time, and dispossess them of their last port in my beat, I sent an expedition to take Georgetown—The *Pawnee* and several other vessels with a Battallion of Marines—[12]

On the 25th I went round the harbor to look at the defences—they were too strong for any fleet that could get at them,—it would have been rediculous to attempt it—even if there had been no obstructions & torpedoes—which however were found abundantly (See my dispatch to Navy Dept with Map of Harbor—& forts—obstructions—torpedoes—published in Annual Report of Navy Depart. 1865. Dec)[13]

With the inadequate force which I had such a measure would have been worse than ridiculous

The expedition to Georgetown was successful,—as soon as the enemy perceived its approach they waited not to give battle, but evacuated—so the Navy had that honor to itself—

I visited the place on the 26th Febr. found its defence very strong and quite sufficient to repel a purely Naval force—Put the town under my own force and officers—who quickly restored order & confidence,—no one was hurt in person or property—[14]

Feeling obliged me to return to Charleston,—on the 1st March steamed out—passing down the channel—early in the morning,—awaiting breakfast and pacing the Cabin came a loud noise,—a shock, everything about me danced,

---

[11] Lt. Charles H. Bradford, USMC, had died on 13 February 1864. Edward W. Callahan, ed., *List of Officers of the Navy of the United States and of the Marine Corps from 1775 to 1900: Comprising a Complete Register of All Present and Former Commissioned, Warranted, and Appointed Officers of the United States Navy, and of the Marine Corps, Regular and Volunteer* (New York: L. R. Hammersly & Co., 1901), 681. Details of his role in the 8 September 1863 assault on Sumter are found in ORN 14: 628–30. See below for details of his reburial ceremony and reinterment.

[12] After learning of the possible evacuation of Battery White at Georgetown, SC, Dahlgren ordered Cmdr. J. Blakeley Creighton and *Mingo* to take the fortification, and sent Marines and *Pawnee* to assist. Creighton wrote Dahlgren on 24 February that he intended to burn the gun carriages and woodwork at the fort in order to destroy it before pushing on to Georgetown itself. ORN 16: 261–62, 268.

[13] *Report of the Secretary of the Navy, with an Appendix Containing Reports from Officers* ([Washington, DC: GPO,] 1865), 253–300. Dahlgren's report of 1 June with diagrams and enclosures is also in ORN 16: 380–429.

[14] Dahlgren wrote, "Battery White, a regular and very strong work . . . had often been represented as a small affair, easily taken . . . It is doubtful whether a strong naval force could have taken it without an ironclad and a land force in reverse." Four companies of Marines occupied the town. ORN 16: 370–71.

that could move,—the front partition was blown in—I thought the boilers had burst,—then the smell of powder was suggestive of an accident to the Magazine—there was a rush of men for the boats—I put on my pea-Coat & Cap—sallied out—there was much consternation—About to ascend the ladder to the upper deck, the great gap in the deck showed it to be the work of a torpedo—The vessel was sinking—a small tug in company to carry orders had paused at sight of the disaster,—was lashed alongside—men, and baggage hurried on board and in a few minutes the "*Harvest Moon*" of the Squadron had set forever—In her I had spent many anxious hours—[15]

Hoisting my flag in another vessel[16] I pursued my way to Charleston and reached there, after some detention on the 4th March

Now the large force which I have commanded for nearly two years must dissolve,—the whole face of things is changed,—if there are enemies before us and around us, they are impotent—

One of another kind however showed its rattle—

On the 7th of February while Sherman & events were marching to a conclusion, and the fabric of rebeldom was falling to ruins around us—pride & joy to every loyal heart,—my eye fell on a copy of Gen. Gillmore's book—I had no time to read,—the country had other work for every man's head & hand—but in turning over its leaves hastily, I saw to my utter astonishment what appeared to me as full confirmation of all the suspicions & warnings that had reached me,—it seemed to me incredible—That and that only undeceived me and led me to decline his proffered hand on my quarter Deck[17]—so much time allowed to elapse after the events, yet every semblance of good feeling—even assurances were not wanting

However as I said,—the country first—there would be time for myself afterwards—

Reaching Charleston, my attention was drawn to a passage in <u>the</u> corre-

[15] One sailor died in the incident. Dahlgren's report, the log of *Harvest Moon*, and a court of inquiry into that vessel's loss are in ORN 16: 282–84.

[16] Dahlgren rode the tug to *Nipsic*; he sailed on it to Charleston Harbor and then made *Philadelphia* his flagship. ORN 16: 371.

[17] When Gillmore visited Dahlgren on 11 February, Dahlgren refused to shake Gillmore's hand, instead offering a bow. Robert J. Schneller Jr., *A Quest for Glory: A Biography of Rear Admiral John A. Dahlgren* (Annapolis, MD: Naval Institute Press, 1996), 307.

spondence[18]—so akin to previous compliments that its source was not to be mistaken—lauding Gen. Gillmore and depreciating myself I addressed at once a note to Gen. Gillmore on the subject and requested that the writer, being within the Military jurisdiction should "be required to refrain from such remarks or leave the Department"

The answer was as sophistical as might be expected,—but in its ceremonious & studied expressions, one only was important—Gen Gillmore saw nothing "in the paragraph which would seem to justify any interference on his part"

He took care to omit the passage laudatory of himself,—

My answer restored the whole as quoted by me—and after reciting as much of the previous letters as might be necessary to keep clear the point in question—I added,—"I feel constrained to say therefore of the remarks alluded to, that so far as they detract from and depreciate myself or the Naval operations they are false and hurtful to the discipline of the Squadron, and as far as they form part of a system of puffing-up and crying-down, are disgraceful to the perpetrator and to any who may seek to be benefitted thereby.

"As it is in your power to prevent the continuance of such remarks and as you decline to do so on the ground that you see nothing in the paragraph sent you to justify that interference, I feel that I have a right to add that whatever remarks of the above character may in future emanate from writers whom you can restrain you render yourself responsible for and can not avoid sharing in the demerit that may attach to them—"[19]

It would be unjust to the character of the reply not to give it in full

"Admiral

I have received your letter of the 7th inst. Although it does not require a reply from me I desire to renew the assurance contained in my letter of the 6th inst. that I hold myself ready at all times to restrain the liberties of correspondents within proper limits, and to ask whether in its execution you are satisfied that you will receive the protection and aid which you desire as expressed in your letter of Febr. 27 or whether in addition thereto you wish me to describe the means I intend to adopt, or to prescribe those means yourself.

[18] On 22 February, the *New York Herald* published an article critical of Dahlgren. The author of it had been attached to Gillmore's staff, but Gillmore denied any involvement with the article. As seen below, Dahlgren believed that Gillmore had been behind the article, based on his own observations as well as a similar incident when Gillmore was under the command of Maj. Gen. Benjamin F. Butler. Ibid., 316–17.

[19] Dahlgren wrote and crossed out here: "The jesuitical character of the reply."

"The insinuations in which you have thought proper to indulge in the last part of your letter I am constrained to pass without notice.

"It is but justice to the officers of my Staff that I should say in their behalf that none of them knew anything of Mr----'s intention to write what he did, or knew that he had written until after its publication.

"It seems needless to add that I never saw or heard of the article until the papers arrived from New York; indeed I did not know that Mr--- continued to write to the New York----- but supposed him to be exclusively engaged in editing a newspaper in Savannah.

Very Respectfully
Your Obed Servt
Q.A. Gillmore Maj. Gen. Com[d]"

Note the reply,—my remarks were directed entirely to his saying that he saw nothing in the article to justify his interference—his letter would lead to the idea that he had said the contrary and intended to interfere—

I said nothing whatever of the officers of his Staff—why does he lug them in?—

However here was my answer

"Sir—In reply to the query contained in yours of the 19 inst.,—I have to say that it is indifferent to me what means you use to suppress the remarks of a public correspondent under your control which are equally at variance with truth so far as I am concerned and derogatory to yourself in permitting them.

"The estimation which attaches to these libels is derived entirely from the fact that the writer is known to be under your control, and therefore what ever he may write carries with it an acquiescence very little less than absolute approval.

"The revival of such remarks just as you resume the command here, has a significance not to be avoided, especially when it is remembered that this same writer and some others indulged in similar remarks during the term of your previous command and that a correspondent affirmed your knowledge and countenance thereof.

"When apprised of this, you entirely denied the allegation, and I frankly accepted that denial, as the charge seemed to me incredible.

"Since that however, this allegation has received confirmation by an officer whose rank and character convey an assurance not to be disposed of by a mere denial.

"In the present instance you say that you 'never saw or heard of the article until the papers arrived from New York'—Perhaps so,—but when it was brought to your notice by me, what did you say then?,—that you saw—'nothing in it to justify your interference'—thus giving more color to the imputations formerly made than I was prepared to expect.

"If this conveys to you the idea that I am seeking your protection, you will learn probably, that it appears differently to others,—my object is to protect myself.

Very Respectfully
Your Obed Serv
J A Dahlgren"

To this letter I never received any answer—the charges contained in it,—or as Gen. Gillmore's previous letter termed such,—the insinuations—are of course unanswered—of course undenied—

This is not the only instance in which Gen. Gillmore has fallen under "insinuations" of a similar character—which too he has been "constrained to pass without notice"—

Gen. Butler's pamphlet in which this subject has been treated, has not that I know of ever been noticed by Gen. Gillmore—The singular coincidence in proclivity to publications of a certain character which Gen. Butler mentions induces me to refer to this pamphlet, a copy of which was sent me by Gen. B.—I shall not attempt to go into the subject in detail—but briefly—

The gist seems to be given in the following passages:—page 12. "Before the order of Sept. 13th was sent, however you (Gen B.) had ascertained with certainty that Chaplain Hudson was the author of certain statements which first appeared in the columns of the *N.Y. Evening Post* on or about the 21st of May 1864, and which were copied into most of the leading journals of the country, which statements reflected very calumniously and unjustly upon your action in the command of your army at the battle of Proctor's creek, in front of Drury's bluff Va. and cited Gen. Gilmore as authority for the criticism."

At page 17—occurs the following extract from the "phonographic notes" of the examination of Mr. Hudson by Gen. Butler.

Q. Do you not know that Gen. Gilmore denied all knowledge of that letter or its author?—
A. Yes sir; I am aware of Gen Gilmore's note to you.
Q. Did not Gen. Gilmore know of your writing that letter before it was sent?
A. I don't know (hesitatingly)
Q. Did he not know of it before it was sent?
A. I think so
Q. Do you not know that he did?
A. Yes Sir

Q. And was not the reason of his sending you away?
A. I can't say that I know it was.
Q. Don't you know that was the reason?
A. I thought at the time that it was.
Q. Had you any doubt in your own mind on the subject?
A. I did not know how necessary the business was that Gen. Gilmore professedly sent me on. I thought that was the reason of his sending me away. I had but little conversation with Gen. Gilmore."
&c &c
On page 18—the following occurs in course of this examination—the Q. I understand to be put like the others by Gen. B—
Q—"You wrote a letter to the press in which you undertook to give your opinion of the conduct of a campaign of which you knew nothing. Then, when stir was made about it, you was sent by Gen. Gilmore to New York on private business for him—yes on pretended business, of which there was no business whatever. There you remained without ever receiving any instructions as to business, nor had you any business there, yet still you remained away till General Gillmore was removed, as [the]—* should have been long before, because this transaction stamps him a —* in addition to being incompetent &c &c"[20]

My only object in referring to this is to show that Gen. Butler complained of Gen. Gillmore' precisely as I have done—Both complaints he seems to have "passed without notice" What reliance then attaches to the unsupported statements of a person who permits such to remain unnoticed.

Of course when a person resorts to such means, his general course is more or less impeached by it,—his statements can never pass into History unless substantiated by other evidence than his own—

It is not my intention to make a full examination of all points made in Gen. Gillmore's Book, or as he calls it—*Report*, particularly those which relate

[20] At the bottom of the page, Dahlgren wrote "* an epithet was used here more forcible than polished," which phrase appears at the foot of the page in the original pamphlet, along with the asterisks.

to myself—[21]which I have always considered as untruly stated, as they have been meanly stated—And I was so occupied when my being assigned to command of the S. Pacific Squadron

That it was idle to attempt to capture Charleston with the force which I had, is indisputably shown by the written opinions of the Lieut. Gen—by that of Commodore Rodgers given on oath—and by the full deliberations of the Council of War—It is impossible to conceive that Gen. Gillmore had any other object in the course he pursued than to cover up his own shortcomings—so far from his undertaking being limited to the destruction of Sumter,—I know that the Navy Department was led to believe "Previous to Gen. Gillmore's departure to assume his present command— that he being "once in possession of Cummings Point could thence reduce Forts Moultrie and Johnson"

The Navy Department informed me that he so stated—

As for the programme which he so clearly puts forth,—it was never received by me,—the orders of the Dep. were merely to cooperate with him and he admits this was done fully—The rest,—his opinion of what the fleet could have done is fully disposed of by the opinions of men, before which his own will not stand for a moment in the estimation of any one whose judgement is worth having—

I know that such discussions are a great scandal to a great cause, but the entire responsibility rests with Gen. Gillmore—not with me, I did my duty to him as a comrade fully, honestly generously,—he has done nothing but deceive me, and attempt to injure me.

On the 16th March, having made the proper arrangements, I had the body of Lieut. Bradford restored to the Cemetery from which it had been so brutally expelled—I sent previously an officer to select the finest site in the ground—service was performed over the body in St Paul's Church by Rev. Mr. Blake the Chaplain of the Squadron—the escort was the largest that could be collected without reference to the rank of the deceased—The Comm. Gen. (Hatch) and myself attended with our numerous Officers of Staff—All the officers of the Army & Navy that could be spared from duty—detachments of Infantry—of Seamen,—a battallion of Marines—Band &c—from the

[21] See Q. A. Gillmore, *Engineer and Artillery Operations Against the Defences of Charleston Harbor in 1863; Comprising the Descent Upon Morris Island, the Demolition of Fort Sumter, the Reduction of Forts Wagner and Gregg. With Observations on Heavy Ordnance, Fortifications, Etc.* (New York: D. Van Nostrand, 1865). Dahlgren worked on various accounts of his career but never published any of them during his life. He did engage in a thorough and extensive examination of the siege of Charleston, along with point-by-point refutations of Gillmore's account, for the historian John William Draper. John William Draper Family Papers, Box 2, Library of Congress.

Church to the Cemetery—and so the Union soldier was duly honored at last[22]

Next day a torpedo exploded under the *Bibb* and nearly did fatal damage—Steam tugs & boats had been employed for some time in removing the rope entanglements & torpedoes,—but some of the latter defied every effort—the *Bibb* was the Coast survey vessel under Captain Boutelle and by my direction was engaged in marking a part of the Channel by which vessels could enter without danger—[23]

Quantities were found ashore ready for use, besides those actually in the water—a number of torpedo boats—

Among other incidents of the many that marked each day of my stay in Charleston I may mention one—The army not being strong enough to spare men I had sent gunboats up the various rivers to preserve order and protect defenceless women & children—this was done and effectually—one day however an occurrence illustrated this & and some of the consequences—best described by brief extracts from a letter from "many ladies of the place" it addresses me thus

"Dear Sir,

"We learn with the deepest regret of the capture of some officers of a tug boat in Cooper River while in the act of protecting and removing helpless women and children from the dangers to which they were exposed on their plantations to a place of safety in town,"—the letter goes on to ask that I will allow them to forward a petition to Richmond—adding "Many others besides ourselves who owe a debt of gratitude to the gunboats would be most happy to sign such a petition and to exert themselves to their utmost to accomplish the release of the gentlemen whose kind efforts to succor the helpless have met with

22 Maj. Gen. John P. Hatch, a member of the class of 1845 at West Point and Mexican-American War veteran, commanded the District of Charleston. *Generals in Blue*, 216–17. John Blake, chaplain of the squadron, officiated. Further details of the ceremony can be found in Madeleine Vinton Dahlgren, *Memoir of John A. Dahlgren: Rear-Admiral United States Navy* (Boston: James R. Osgood and Company, 1882), 505.

23 Assistant Charles O. Boutelle, U.S. Coast Survey, reported that the torpedo "exploded under our port bow about midway between the port guard and fore channels . . . Sixty fathoms of studded mooring chains, 1½ inch diameter, coiled upon the port side of the vessel forward, were thrown across the deck. The knees upon the port side are started out, and the joiner work shows signs of the blow received." ORN 16: 295.

so unfortunate a return &c[24]

I mention this on my own behalf and of the Navy to show the kind of treatment which prisoners & families met with from me,—though laboring under the strongest provocation that could drive a man to forget himself, I never failed to extend to them the most humane treatment—

Towards the middle of April I had a letter from my friend Gen. Sherman then at Goldsboro. N.C. speaking at length of his progress—[25]

Gen. Schimmelfennig also took leave and I was happy to afford him a passage in the Navy Supply steamer—He is since gone to another life—peace to him he was a gallant & faithful soldier of the Union—highly skilled in his vocation—disease had stricken him hard,—but though hardly able to mount his horse he persevered to the last, and with myself was the first officer of rank to enter Charleston—May the Country not forget the family of this brave man, who from a foreign land, became one of us—honor to his memory—[26]

April 14th was a great day—the national flag which had been hauled down by rebels on that day, was again hoisted Rev. Mr. Beecher delivered a fine discourse Many were there,—none more deservedly than a remnant of the Naval Column which had endeavored to master it in Septem. 1863—I had them collected from the Squadron under the command of Capt. Williams[27] who was at their head, was captured—kept close prisoner at Columbia, and even ironed for some weeks—so the right prevails at last—[28]

On the 19th came to us the sad news of the death of our noble President by the hands of a detestable assassin sorrow entered into every heart—God help those who are more guilty of this thing than the vile perpetrator,—who

---

[24] Four men had been captured on 22 March 1865 while "on shore for the purpose of assisting some of the white families against the negroes at Lewisfield." The men captured were Acting Ensign Charles H. Hanson, Acting Master's Mate Henry Lynch, Acting Third Assistant Engineer William H. Barclay, and Acting Third Assistant Engineer John Ryan. See ORN 16: 297. This letter likely references this episode.

[25] Letter not found.

[26] Schimmelfennig, suffering from tuberculosis, took sick leave on 8 April 1865. He died on 9 September 1865 in Pennsylvania. Warner, *Generals in Blue*, 424.

[27] Lt. Cmdr. Edward P. Williams.

[28] On the fourth anniversary of the evacuation of Fort Sumter, the same flag lowered before the evacuation was raised again by Maj. Gen. Robert Anderson, who had been in command during the evacuation. During the ceremony, portions of Psalms 126, 47, 98 and 20 were read, followed by the raising of the flag along with a salute of 100 guns from Sumter. After the salute, bands played the Star Spangled Banner and Reverend Henry Ward Beecher delivered an address. "Programme of the Order of Exercises at the Re-Raising of the United States Flag, on Fort Sumter, Charleston, S.C.," John Adolphus Bernard Dahlgren Papers, Library of Congress.

Admiral John A. Dahlgren and staff. Glass negative, c. 1865.

Brady Photograph Collection, National Archives, B-64.

have preached & talked of such a resort until their tool was nerved to his work—At once our flags drooped to half mast and I ordered minute guns from every ship—[29]

The same mail[30] brought me tidings from the War Dept. that the remains of my gallant son had been recovered and would be brought to Washington May 2[d]—we have official news that Gen Johnson has surrendered to Gen Sherman—And so ends the great Drama—[31]

Next day much gratified at the appearance of Gen. Sherman who arrived in

[29] Dahlgren announced Lincoln's assassination in General Order 39. In it, he gave instructions that "twenty-one minute guns will be fired from every vessel in the squadron, beginning with the senior vessel, each vessel following in order of seniority. The minute guns will be repeated at sunset." He also ordered the officers of the squadron to "wear crape on the left arm." ORN 16: 318–19. He later wrote the Navy Department, informing them of "a sensation of indignation and grief as universal as it was profound and sincere, far exceeding anything I have before witnessed." He also explained his course of action, noting that it "has been in excess of regulations." ORN 16: 319–20.

[30] The mail arrived aboard the steamer *Fulton*.

[31] On 26 April 1865, Confederate Gen. Joseph E. Johnston surrendered his forces, the last major field army of the Confederacy, to Maj. Gen. William T. Sherman at Bennett Place, NC.

a Steamer—after an interesting & private interview—and a peep ashore he left for the North—[32]

Soon after came tidings of capture of Jefferson Davis—he was sent North under convoy of one of my Steamers, the *Tuscarora*—[33]

On the 23[d] May I had the satisfaction of sending North the only and the finest Charleston Ram saved from the Rebels,—the *Columbia*: the other five at Charleston had been blown up or burned—The *Columbia* had been bilged and sunk—but I had her raised—fitted her and now she departs for Norfolk—[34]

May ends and the Navy Depart directs the scale of reduction of my force—all right—When this is done I am to turn over what is left and return home—

On the 17th of June having made all the necessary arrangements and sent home nearly all the vessels of the squadron I transferred my flag to the *Pawnee* and departed—The Military Com. Gen. Hatch came alongside to say good bye—and I turned my back on the scene that for two years had evoked all my energies—

After a pleasant passage the *Pawnee* anchored in the Potomac off Washington—there the President[35] with some of his Cabinet visited the *Pawnee* and on the 12th I struck my flag as Admiral of the South Atlantic Blockading Squadron The seal of official judgement was thus set on my command of two years—the most numerous command for the same length of time ever held by any US. Naval Officer—

The Navy Department in the order closing my command of the South Atlantic Blockading Squadron says:—

"In relieving you from a command which you have conducted with ability and energy for two years, the Department takes the occasion to express to you its appreciation of your services, and of the services of those who have been asso-

---

32 Sherman arrived aboard the steamer *Russia*. Dahlgren in his diary entry of 3 May noted, "His flag is a jack with 'S' in it." ORN 16:373.

33 Capt. Charles W. Pickering, commanding *Tuscarora*, convoyed the steamer *Clyde*, which carried former Confederate President Jefferson Davis, his wife Varina Davis, former Vice President of the Confederacy Alexander H. Stephens, and former Confederate Postmaster John H. Reagan, among others. See ORN 16:334.

34 Fleet Engineer Robert Danby had raised the rebel ram on Dahlgren's instruction. Dahlgren reported to the Navy Department that "the *Columbia* appears to be a finer and larger vessel than any of the rebel rams." He noted her 6-inch plating, length of 216 feet, breadth of 51 feet, and armament of 6 guns. ORN 16:336. In his diary entry of 26 March he described the Confederate vessel as "a remarkably fine, powerful vessel...a really formidable customer, and very strongly built." ORN 16: 372.

35 Andrew Johnson.

ciated with you in the efficient blockade of the coast and harbors of a central and important position of the Union, and in the work of repossessing the Forts and restoring the authority and supremacy of the Government in the Insurgent States."[36]

Now ought I to omit what I value equally the voluntary testimony of our distinguished Captain—Sherman—In his testimony before the Congressional Committee on the Conduct of the War he thus speaks with his characteristic unreserve:—

"On the morning of May 3^{d} we ran into Charleston Harbor where I had the pleasure to meet Admiral Dahlgren, who had in all my previous operations from Savannah Northward aided me with a constancy and manliness that commanded my entire respect and deep affection."[37]

I had aided Gen. Gillmore with the same spirit—Contrast the unbiased, voluntary testimony of the great genius & true man with the pitiful, sneaking evasions and meanness of the other!—the "king of shreds and patches"—[38]

My first duty on being freed from official duties, was to the remains and the memory of my gallant son Ulric Dahlgren—they had been brought from their resting place near Richmond as soon as within the lines of the U.S Army, to Washington by order of the War Department and placed in the Vault of the Congressional Cemetery—no doubt could exist in regard to their being really the true remains,—but to make sure I caused the Iron casket to be opened and the report satisfied me,—it was out of my power to be present myself—impossible to look upon the sad sight.

The heat of the weather made it advisable to defer the funeral rites until cool weather—

On the last day of October, the body reposed in the Council Chamber of the City—surrounded by good & true Union officers—covered by the flag which he had so well served—

It was but a short distance to the Church—every spot alive with memories of former days—every spot of the ground that was trodden by the solemn proces-

---

36 *Annual Report of the Secretary of the Navy* ([Washington, DC: Government Printing Office,] 1865), 347. For the entire 23 June 1865 letter of Gideon Welles thanking Dahlgren for his efforts and relieving him of command of the South Atlantic Blocking Squadron, see Ibid., 346–47.

37 From documents Sherman submitted to the Joint Committee on the Conduct of the War. *JCCW* 6: "Sherman-Johnston," 12.

38 From *Hamlet*, Act III, Scene 4. Hamlet uses the lines to refer to Claudius, his treacherous uncle who had murdered Hamlet's father and married his mother, Gertrude.

sion had been pressed over and over by his young feet—his cold body was borne close by the door of the dwelling where he had passed most of his brief life—from the windows now crowded with sympathizing spectators, had been witnessed day by day his boyish outgoings and incomings—The Church which was to witness the parting services had held him each sabbath as it came—The occasion was one not easily forgotten—in the great assembly were, President & Cabinet—Officers of all degrees—fathers, mothers, daughters—Mr Beecher[39] spoke with the fervor & eloquence that was so truly his own—

From Washington the body was transported to Philad. and laid in the Hall of Independence—few have that honor—the last before was the honored President Lincoln—There a discourse was pronounced by the Rev. J.P. Wilson remarkable & powerful—It was he who first bestowed the benediction of the Church in baptism—on Ulric Dahlgren then a little nestling infant and well he remembered it—

Followed the escort to the grave—amid notes of solemn music and glittering bayonets—The Com. General was there[40]—him that he now followed was one of his staff at Gettysburg—had captured dispatches from the rebel President in one of those bold swoops that he was wont to make like a young eagle and brought them to Headqrs—while the battle was going on—that night his way was across the battlefield, and his footsteps had been carefully guarded from the dying & dead that loaded the ground—now he has joined that great Army too!—

Softly he was laid, just by his mother—along the banks where the Schuylkill is loveliest—Noble boy you will not be forgotten—

I returned home and sat down to muse over the events of four years service against a mighty rebellion and to prepare such notes as seemed worth preserving—

39 Reverend Henry Ward Beecher.

40 Maj. Gen. George Gordon Meade.

CHAPTER 7

After the War, 1866

1866

In Febry I was a member of a joint Board to consider the defences of our harbors—Gen. Gillmore had been detailed as a member—but I declined to serve with him—he was detached It was my misfortune to serve once with him,—it would have been my fault, a second time—

In May the Dep[t] named me as President of the Board of Visitors to the Naval School at Annapolis

Towards the end of September the Department assigned me command of the South Pacific Squadron, for which I shall leave New York on the 1st Decem. next—

And so you have a hasty view of the events of my life—written in some haste,—but more especially the latter part,—which I have been compelled to pass over too rapidly—

I should have mentioned that toward the end of 1863 The Union League of Philadelphia sent me their silver Medal with a handsome letter—

You will find much assistance in making your outline,—from various public Documents—

1st

The Annual Reports of the Navy Department to Congress 1861 to 1866—

2[d]

My official dispatches given with these Reports—there is a plan of Charleston Harbor in that of 1865—(the last) and drawings of its defences very complete—

3[d]

Report on "Heavy Ordnance" by Committee on Conduct of War made early in 1864—and made a great error too in one respect too—when they said "But the Dahlgren guns of the largest calibre are now being manufactured upon the

Rodman principle"[1]—because they would lead one to suppose that it applied to the Cannon forming the chiefly the Armament of the Navy, viz the XI inch and IX inch Cannon—whereas it applies only to the few XV inch cannon in the Monitors, which in the haste of arming during a Civil War, there was no time to test in any other way—

My views are however fully borne out in regard to Rifle Cannon & Wrought iron cannon—not by the Report but by facts—the bursting at Fort Fisher settled one and notwithstanding the conclusions[2] of the Board on One wrought iron cannon, Gen. Gillmore being Chief of it, no other proved like it,—the ignorance of the subject being shown in drawing conclusions from one as to others that will serve for cast iron.—but not for wrought iron

4th

My Report on operations off Charleston made to Committee on Conduct of War June 1864—in which it will be perceived I was still in the dark as to when Gillmore was burrowing[3]

5th

My Report on Monitors—Jan 1864 in the Navy Dept Report on Armored Vessels—1864.[4]

Writings of various professional men refer to my opinions and doings—Gen. Barnard (U.S) on Defences of New York[5]

Gen. Bormann (Belgian) to my Ordnance &c[6]

1 The report of the Joint Committee on the Conduct of the War referenced here can be found in JCCW 5, "Heavy Ordnance," 1-179. Rodman's method involved casting the gun with water circulating in the core to cool the metal.

2 Dahlgren wrote and crossed out: "absurd" before "conclusions."

3 Dahlgren's letter to the Joint Committee on the Conduct of the War concerning operations at Charleston is found in JCCW 6, "Miscellaneous," 1-11.

4 Dahlgren provided a comprehensive statement on the merits of the Monitors to the Department of the Navy. *Report of the Secretary of the Navy in Relation to Armored Vessels* (Washington, DC: Government Printing Office, 1864), 579–88.

5 J[ohn] G. Barnard, *The Dangers and Defences of New York. Addressed to the Hon. J. B. Floyd, Secretary of War* (New York: D. Van Nostrand, 1859).

6 Charles G. Bormann, best known for his timed fuse designs. Spencer Tucker, *Arming the Fleet: U.S. Navy Ordnance in the Muzzle-Loading Era* (Annapolis, MD: Naval Institute Press, 1989), 244.

Grivel (French)—also the principal Ordnance writers, French & English[7]

Engineer King inscribed to me his work on Steam[8]—Capt Parker of the Navy inscribed his work on Artillery[9]—(By the way I should have mentioned him on commanding the Naval Battery that I placed on Morris I. to help batter Sumter)[10]

I hope I shall be pardoned for this disquisition on myself and my service—[11]but you have asked me and I answer as if you had placed me on the witness Stand

Presentation copies of Dahlgren's books: (L to R) *Practice of the Experimental Battery*, *Shells and Shell Guns*, and *Boat Armament of the U.S. Navy*.

Naval History and Heritage Command, Navy Department Library.

---

7 Baron Louis Antoine Richild Grivel, a French ordnance specialist, wrote about floating batteries. His main work was *Attaques et bombardements maritime avant et pendant la guerre d'Orient. Sébastopol.—Bomarsund.—Odessa—Sweaborg.—Kinburn*, 2nd ed. (Paris: J. Dumaine, 1857). English authority Sir Howard Douglas mentioned Dahlgren and his writings in a revised edition of his manual on naval gunnery. Sir Howard Douglas, *A Treatise on Naval Gunnery*, 5th ed., rev. (London: John Murray, 1860).

8 U.S. Navy Chief Engineer James Wilson King.

9 Parker dedicated *The Naval Howitzer Ashore* (New York: D. Van Nostrand, 1865) to Dahlgren.

10 On 22 July 1863, Dahlgren ordered then-Cmdr. Foxhall Parker to command a detachment of two Whitworth rifles and two Parrott rifles served by a naval crew. ORN 14:385.

11 Dahlgren wrote and crossed out: "egotism from one end to the other."

APPENDIX 1

Letter of William T. Sherman to John A. Dahlgren

"Copy."

Headquarters Military Division
of the Mississippi
St. Louis, Mo., Feb. 14. 1866.

Rear Admiral Dahlgren,
U.S. Navy. Washington, D.C.

Admiral—

I have the honor to acknowledge the receipt of your communication of Feb. 3, asking my judgments on certain points relating to the operations of our land and Naval forces about Charleston in the year 1863. I have before me the map you were kind enough to send, and from a residence at Fort Moultrie during the years 1842-3-4-5 and 6, I had acquired a knowledge of the water and land round about Charleston Harbor, and therefore feel competent to express an opinion on the points you make.

To your first question I answer,—I would not have advised you to run the Iron-clad Fleet past Fort Sumter into the inner Harbor of Charleston on the theory that by bringing the city under your guns, the enemy would have evacuated both City and Forts. I dont believe the Forts would have been evacuated, but that the Fleet would have been subjected to a terrific fire from the circle of batteries, that would have crippled every ship and rendered the Fleet useless for other purposes. The enemy could well have afforded to exchange the city of Charleston for the Fleet.

To the second question I answer that of course the passage of the Iron-clad Fleet into the inner harbor before Gen. Gillmore had reduced Battery Wagner would have been still more imprudent.

To the third question I answer that, had you run into the inner Harbor, and up Cooper River, the enemy could easily have held all his works on James and Sullivan's Islands without trouble, as the fire of your ships could not reach the roads from the interior to these Islands. The enemy could have still held all his shore batteries, and you would have been compelled to run out for supplies.

When you and I were in Savannah about Christmas of 1864, we discussed freely all these points, and you will recall my opinions then expressed most emphatically.

1st, That Charleston was a place of no military importance at all,—that the labor spent in the attempt to reduce it was useless,—that all the attacks from the sea front were playing into the hands of the enemy, who of course had reason to rejoice at every attack from that quarter.

2nd, We had no use for Charleston unless an Army were at hand strong enough to act independently in the Interior, and when such an Army was at hand, Charleston was perfectly easy of capture, with all its torpedoes, land batteries and Sea forts by the occupation of the Interior, from Port Royal or Bull's Bay.

3rd. That fleets, whether of Iron-clads or wooden ships, should only engage land batteries when they have a vast superiority of Artillery. Had you put your Fleet inside of Charleston Harbor, your twenty heavy guns would have been the target for some of the heaviest calibre in the world and of the most approved pattern. You would have lost the Fleet, and at best have only damaged the City of Charleston a little more than was committed by the rebels themselves on evacuation.

I now thank you in person for not having made the hazardous experiment, for when the time did come to act seriously, your fleet was perfect, well manned, and admirably suited to aid me in the execution of the plan which did accomplish the fall of Charleston, and more too.

With great respect,
Your friend,
W. T. Sherman,
Maj. Gen.

Copy, John Adolphus Bernard Dahlgren Papers, Library of Congress. Dahlgren also copied portions of this letter in a manuscript he sent to John William Draper; John William Draper Family Papers, Box 2, Library of Congress.

APPENDIX 2

Description of Defenses of Charleston Harbor

Note Defences of Harbor

The general contour of Charleston Harbor may be likened to that of a bottle—

At its mouth are the Forts Moultrie and Sumter

Fort Moultrie with its adjacent batteries stands on Sullivans I, at the right when entering—

Fort Moultrie itself looks directly across the entrance while the batteries extending from its left overlap and not only cross fire with Moultrie but look down the channel by which vessels approach. The works extending from the right of Moultrie cross fire with the others upon the entrance and overlapping command the channel passing into the harbor from the entrance—

The whole length of these works is nearly one mile and a half along the beach of the island and as close to the water as practicable—

There are three principal batteries viz;—Fort Moultrie in the centre, Fort Beauregard on its left and Battery Bee on its right—

Fort Moultrie as it existed previously to the rebellion was built of brick and armed with 24 pdrs, 32 pdrs and some 10" Columbiads—unsupported by contiguous batteries. In that condition it was too feeble to resist any serious attack by ironclads.

But when the operations began on Morris I. in 1863—its brick walls had been encased with earth & sand nearly 25 feet thick—smooth & rifled cannon of the heaviest calibers mounted and protected by traverses of great thickness—Bee & Beauregard were not inferior in defensive power—and were heavily armed, the former with fewer guns—These three principal batteries were connected by lines which included other batteries such as Batteries Marion, Rutledge &c all powerfully constructed and armed—

As the shore line of Sullivans I. eastward of Beauregard was not approachable by vessels of force—it was only covered by some small detached batteries to interdict landing. But the extremity of the island seaward being only separated from Long I. by a narrow inlet—was protected by a very heavy work known as Fort Marshall—which never came into play as no attack was made from this quarter, as might have been done if the General had been willing—

On the examination of these works after their capture in 1865 we found them to be most carefully and skilfully constructed nothing was wanting that could contribute to their defensive, capacity while 67 pieces of various kinds were mounted—smooth & rifled cannon, some of 8" and 10" calibre mortars &c

The powers of this line of works was thoroughly tested on the 8th of Septem[r] 1863, when I sent up the *Ironsides* and Monitors to cover the *Weehawken* then aground—the action last for three hours, until the *Ironsides* had but 30 shells left—There were three or four guns dismounted in Moultrie and some forty men killed or wounded, but no impression of importance made on the works, so that they renewed their fire on the *Weehawken* when she attempted to float a few hours later in the day—On the other hand the Monitors were much battered

Opposite to Sullivans I. with its formidable works stands Fort Sumter at a distance of about one mile—It is placed on the edge of the shoal water that bounds the channel on that side

At the first of the rebellion it constituted the principal defence of the entrance—as Fort Moultrie was then the only work on the opposite side and also very feeble for offense or defense—

This state of things was changed entirely at the time of the joint operation—Moultrie had been converted into an earthwork and extended on each side as already described until it was no longer susceptible of manpower—And the course of our operations in July & August 1863 worked no less important changes in the character of Sumter—

As soon as the Union forces had captured the works on the South end of Morris I. and occupied that island to musket shot of Wagner, the rebel authorities quickly discerned that the loss of the whole island must follow and in all probability Sumter would also fall into our hands—It was only a question of time when these events would occur and their purpose was to delay this as long as possible, so as to substitute for Sumter proper works inside, and also to remove from it, the numerous guns with which it was armed and which they could not afford to lose—

Gen. Ripley who was in immediate charge of the defences reports officially on the 21' Aug. 1863—"the heavy guns and Mortars which have been received and secured from Fort Sumter have been placed in position &c"[1]

General Gillmore's opinions varied,—the published from the unpublished In a letter to me (official dated 23[d] August[)] he admits that "Some of the guns from the gorge and the adjacent face looking towards Cumming's Points were doubtless removed to James and Sullivan's I. before the bombardment commenced or during its progress"[2]

When he came to publish his opinions more than a year after the events to which they refer he found it convenient to say—"some time elapsed before any of its (Sumter's) guns were mounted by the enemy at other points in the harbor."[3]—He could not deny that they had been removed but with that jesuitical discrimination which he so constantly exercises, he only says they were not mounted. Now so far as reasoning on ordinary premises was concerned the difficulty lay in being able to remove them from Sumter—that once accomplished it was a mere question of labor to mount them in places less exposed. This was a matter which we were competent to judge of as probable from outside—And it appears from subsequent information contained in Gen. Ripley's reports that the judgment was correct. Even the probable direction of our efforts, previous to actual development seems to have influenced the rebels to anticipate possible consequences; for a British officer who visited Sumter in June says,—"the guns have been removed from the casemates on the eastern face."[4]

The success of the rebels in protracting the defence of Fort Wagner accomplished the main purpose and enabled them to effect a complete substitution for Sumter—In the two months elapsing between the day of our landing and Septr. 6th they had given to Fort Johnson all the strength that was desirable and other works in system with it—

They also learned by experience that the loss of Sumter was not a necessary consequence to the loss of Morris I. and were able to hold it after losing its

[1] Ripley's report has been published. For the quotation see OR 28, Part I: 390. The full report appears at Ibid., 284–92.

[2] For the complete letter, see OR 28, Part 2: 56.

[3] See Q. A. Gillmore, *Engineer and Artillery Operations Against the Defences of Charleston Harbor in 1863; Comprising the Descent Upon Morris Island, the Demolition of Fort Sumter, the Reduction of Forts Wagner and Gregg. With Observations on Heavy Ordnance, Fortifications, Etc.* (New York: D. Van Nostrand, 1865), 65.

[4] The British visitor was Arthur James Lyon Fremantle, a lieutenant colonel of the Coldstream Guards. He also noted that "the lower tier of casements has been filled up with earth to give extra strength, and prevent the balls from coming right through into the interior of the work, which happened at the last attack." [Arthur James Lyon] Fremantle, *Three Months in the Southern States: April–June, 1863* (New York: John Bradburn, 1864), 182.

artillery power as a first class work—and to convert it into a species of outpost to Forts Johnson & Moultrie where a garrison could defend the obstructions of the entrance that were nearest, with musketry and light artillery—and even a few heavy cannon in the lower casemates—

Fort Johnson then offered itself to ships entering as the principal substitute for Sumter—

Supposing that our vessels succeeded in braving the fire of Sullivans I. and removing or forcing the obstructions, the Main channel would lead them to turn sharply to the left and steer nearly for Fort Johnson—receiving its fire ahead and that of Sullivans I. astern—Sumter being the pivot of the movement—On this track lay the three large torpedoes, with some 2000^{lbs} of powder in each—

The Fort Johnson which our vessels were to encounter was a series of earthworks constructed like those of Sullivans I. in the best manner—with strong traverses and a large bomb proof—armed with 12 of the heaviest cannon, smooth and rifled, 8^{in} and ten Inch; whilst near it on a sand spit running out towards Morris I. and armed with Six heavy pieces, were some detached batteries.

In view of the whole tenor of Gillmore's book, his failure to represent these works properly, subjects him to the imputation of misrepresentation as to their real strength—

At page 10. §.9. after describing Fort Moultrie as a brick work with a tier of 24 pdr. 32 pdrs. and some 8^{inch} Columbiads <u>en barbette</u> (that is looking over the top of the wall) he says—"Strong earthworks were erected on the upper and lower ends, as well as at intermediate points of both Morris and Sullivan's islands. § 10—Additional guns were mounted on Fort Moultrie and it was otherwise materially strengthened."[5]

Compare this flippant statement with the impressions of Wagner which are conveyed generally in his Report but were particularly in §82 and §168[6]—and let any officer who has had to deal with these works say how far they are justified—Our ironclads almost silenced Wagner when they engaged it seriously—while they could only quell the batteries of Sullivans I. at the cost of great damage to themselves and only attempted it under urgent necessity—Wagner was

---

5 Dahlgren has garbled his citations here. The description of Moultrie appears in §5. The quotations come from §8 and §9. Gillmore, *Engineer and Artillery Operations*, 8–9.

6 In §82, Gillmore remarked on "the truly formidable character of the armament of Fort Wagner, its hidden resources, and the great strength and capacity of its bomb-proof shelter." In §168, Gillmore wrote, "Fort Wagner was found to be a work of the most formidable character—far more so, indeed, than the most exaggerated statements of prisoners and deserters had led us to expect." Ibid., 35, 74.

insignificant compared to the Sullivan's I. batteries and scarcely equal to any one of them singly—

Of Fort Johnson he says "Old Fort Johnson on James I. was rebuilt and armed with a few heavy guns and mortars."[7]

The old Fort Johnson was never rebuilt—it was an affair of past times, and in 1826 the Chief Engineer speaks of "the few remains of old Fort Johnson."[8] Much less must have been extant in 1861, the new works were of earth, nearer to the shore line and conforming to its contour—heavily armed and protected by traverses with a large bomb proof—The character of the works was as dissimilar as their strength—The old Fort would have been knocked down in an hour by any respectable ship of war of this day—The new works would have matched our ironclads, and could not have been disabled by them—

About 1300 yds. above Johnson is battery Wampler, a small but very strong earth-work armed with two 10^{inch} Columbiads

And at a like distance further was Battery Glover—a strong earth work armed with three 8 inch rifled Cannon—

Opposite to these works, and on the other side of the Main Channel were Fort Ripley—a crib-work on a shoal,—with two cannon—and Castle Pinckney with 3 of 10 inch and a seven inch rifle—

Forming with Battery Glover and Castle Pinckney the apex of a triangle was White Point—the extreme projecting point of the peninsula on which is located Charleston: bearing nearly the same relation to the Harbor that the Battery at N.Y. does to its harbor.

White Point was edged by a line of earth works, very strongly constructed,—perhaps more so than any other in the harbor—and armed with an English 700pdr—3 of 11^{inch}. One ten Inch and an 8^{in} rifle.

On either hand from White Point flows the Cooper and Ashly rivers. On the wharves at small distances are detached earth works known as Batteries Waring, Vanderhorst, Laurens, Calhoun, armed with the heaviest calibres, among them the other 700pdr rifle, for which we were indebted to the kindness of our English friends—

It is not merely the individual power of these works that conveys a fair impression of their capacity to defend the harbor—but the manner also in which they were bound up into a system, so that no one of them could be attacked with-

[7] From §11. Ibid., 9.

[8] From Chief Engineer Totten's report of 1826, portions of which were reprinted in a report of the House Committee on Military Affairs on fortifications in 1862. "Permanent Fortifications and Sea-Coast Defences," House Report 86, 37th Congress, 2d Session, 43.

out being subjected to the fire of others from different directions and at effective range—and as the vessels proceeded this network of batteries became closer—

On arriving at the edge of the shoal extending from White Point where the main channel branches into the Ashley and Cooper Rivers a vessel would be under fire from Batteries Wampler and Glover—Fort Ripley—White Point—Castle Pinckney—Batteries Vanderhorst and Frazier,—coming from all directions ahead, astern and abeam and at effective distances—with no alternative except,—to go on so as to pass beyond the fire, or to withdraw from the harbor or to silence the batteries—

1. To pass beyond the batteries, it would be necessary to go up the Cooper River some distance—leaving it in the power of the enemy to block the channel behind so as to cut off all chance of return—

2d To withdraw, would be to effect nothing after the loss and exposure of entering—

3d To silence the batteries, would require more ships than were at my command or perhaps at that of the Navy Department.

This is not mere opinion—the resistance of Fort Wagner furnishes facts—Its offensive power bore no comparison to that of Moultrie, Bee, Beauregard, Johnson, White Point &c But its construction was of the same character and material—Now let us note what it endured. On the 10th July four Monitors began by pounding it all day at fair range—they continued next day, and on the 18th the *Ironsides* frigate and five Monitors battered the work, whilst 41 light pieces assisted from the land batteries—an assault in force by Gillmore followed and was repulsed with severe loss to us. By the 23d of August, the ironclads and Gunboats had cannonaded Wagner on twenty five occasions, besides the work done by the cannon of the land works.

The work was abandoned on the 6th of Septem. immediately previous to which it was subjected to a heavy fire from our batteries and ships.

Col. Turner Chief of Artillery reports to Gillmore that on the 5th Septr. Fort Wagner was opened on from the land batteries with one 10 inch (300)pdr. Rifle, four 8inch (200pdr.) rifles, nine 100 pdr. rifles, Ten 30 pdr. rifles, Ten 10inch Mortars &c which continued all day and next day—At the same time the *Ironsides* and Monitors maintained a flank fire from Six XVinch–Eleven XIinch guns and three 8inch (150pdr.) rifles—

Gillmore himself thus describes this cannonade;—"These final operations against Fort Wagner were actively inaugurated at the break of day on the morning of Septr. 5th. For forty two consecutive hours the spectacle presented was of surpassing sublimity and grandeur. Seventeen siege and coehorn mortars unceasingly dropped their shells into the work over the heads of our sappers and the guards of the advanced trenches: 13 of our heavy Parrott Rifles, 100, 200 and

300 pdrs, pounded away at short though regular intervals at the SW. angle of the bomb-proof while during the day time the *New Ironsides* with remarkable regularity and precision kept almost incessant stream of XI inch shells from her 8-gun broadside."

What was the condition of Wagner after all this?

Col. Turner reports (146)—"Notwithstanding the heavy fire of this bombardment together with all the fire Fort Wagner had been subject to since the commencement of our attack from land and naval batteries, its defences were not materially injured"—"Our fire of rifle shells on the 5th and 6th insts. at the bombproof did little or no damage."[9]

General Seymour who gallantly led the assaults on Wagner on the 11th and 18th of July says,—"the effect of the firing ashore as well as afloat, was practically nothing in disturbing the defensive capacities of Wagner"—"The symetry of the work was somewhat disarranged,—nothing more &c"[10]

The armament of Wagner suffered as little permanent injury as the work itself—

Gen. Gillmore thus expresses himself §240. page 118—"It reflects no discredit upon our Navy, to say that Fort Wagner, with its garrison covered as it was by a secure bombproof and with facilities for keeping its supplies of men, ammunition and guns unimpaired, could never have been reduced by a naval force or any other means than those adopted viz;—by sapping up to the ditch of the work and then assaulting or threatening an assault from the advanced trenches."[11]

Now compare the advantages of any of the principal interior works of the harbor with those of Wagner—the latter was the outermost work of the rebel position—with no support except such as was possible from the distant fire of James I. or of the gorge of Sumter—The vessels could approach and leave at pleasure—The works inside formed a system with each other; no one of them could be reached except at great risk and withdrawal might be impracticable after defeat

To attack any one was to be subjected to the fire of several others—and under the circumstances this was to have been done by the vessels alone; the army was avowedly powerless to draw a line against a single one of these numerous batteries—or to land one man or all upon Sullivans I. or James I. Together, the troops & ships had reduced an isolated outpost in two months,—what could the

[9] Gillmore includes Turner's entire report of 8 September 1863 in his book. Gillmore, *Engineer and Artillery Operations*, 135–47.

[10] Dahlgren quoted these statements in his official report of 16 October 1865. ORN 16:437.

[11] Gillmore, *Engineer and Artillery Operations*, 118–19.

vessels alone effect against a series of more powerful works individually sustaining each other!

Col. Freemantle of the British Army looking from Fort Sumter on the 9th June 1863—says—"In fact both sides of the Harbor for several miles appear to bristle with forts mounting heavy guns."[12]

Besides the Main Channel there were two others, Hog. I and Folly I. Channel, but they were shallow narrow & winding among shoals so as to be impracticable for the ironclads or for any vessel of War—Yet they were obstructed by piles, by obstructions and covered by batteries at Mr. Pleasants and Haddwell's Point—

The mouth of the Ashley was obstructed by a frame of heavy timber pointed with torpedoes—not removeable under fire—

In addition to these defences there were three ironclad rams, mounting in all 14 heavy guns, most of them rifled—These vessels were like the rebel Ram *Merrimac*—and quite as powerful though perhaps not so long—They were not to be omitted as a serviceable element in the defence in connection with the batteries—

With this description of the works about the Harbor of Charleston may be associated the opinions of officers already cited in this paper—particularly that of the Council of Officers in October 1863—Unanimously that "Forts Moultrie & Johnson could not be reduced by the force present of ironclads, unsupported by the Army"

May 10th 1869—

[12] Fremantle, *Three Months in the Southern States*, 184

BIBLIOGRAPHY

Archival Sources

Library of Congress, Washington, DC
John Adolphus Bernard Dahlgren Papers, 1794–1889.
John William Draper family papers, 1777–1951.

Navy Department Library, Washington, DC
John A. Dahlgren Autobiography

Published Sources

Abbott, John S. C. "Charles Ellet and His Naval Steam Rams," *Harper's New Monthly Magazine* No. 189 (February 1866) :295-312.

Acts and Resolutions of the Third Session of the Thirty-Seventh Congress, begun on Monday, December 1, 1862 and Ended on Wednesday, March 4, 1863. Washington, D.C.: Government Printing Office, (1863).

Barnard, J[ohn] G. *The Dangers and Defences of New York. Addressed to the Hon. J. B. Floyd, Secretary of War*. New York: D. Van Nostrand, 1859.

Beale, Howard K., ed. *The Diary of Edward Bates 1859–1866*. Washington, DC: Government Printing Office, 1933.

Browning, Robert M., Jr. *Success Is All that Was Expected: The South Atlantic Blockading Squadron during the Civil War*. Washington, DC: Brassey's, 2002.

Butler, Benjamin F. *Official Documents Relating to a "Chaplain's Campaign (Not) with General Butler," but in New York*. Lowell, MA: Charles Hunt, 1865.

Callahan, Edward W., ed. *List of Officers of the Navy of the United States and of the Marine Corps from 1775 to 1900: Comprising a Complete register of All Present and Former Commissioned, Warranted, and Appointed Officers of the United States Navy, and of the Marine Corps, Regular and Volunteer*. New York: L. R. Hammersly & Co., 1901.

Cheng, Eileen Ka-May. *The Plain and Noble Garb of Truth: Nationalism and Impartiality in American Historical Writing, 1784–1860*. Athens: University of Georgia Press, 2008.

Clay, Cassius M. *Cassius Marcellus Clay: Memoirs, Writings, and Speeches*. Volume 1. Cincinnati: J. Fletcher Brennan & Co., 1886.

Coston, Marth J. *A Signal Success: The Work and Travels of Mrs. Martha J. Coston: An Autobiography*. Philadelphia: J. B. Lippincott, 1886.

Cutrer, Thomas W. *Ben McCullough and the Frontier Military Tradition*. Chapel Hill: University of North Carolina Press, 1993.

Dahlgren, John A. *An Account of the Experiments Made in the French Navy for the Trial of Bomb Cannon, etc. By H. J. Paixhans, Lieut. Colonel of Artillery*. Philadelphia: E. G. Dorsey, 1838.

———. *Boat Armament of the U.S. Navy*, 2nd Ed. Philadelphia: King and Baird, 1856.

———. *Memoir of Ulric Dahlgren*. Philadelphia: J. B. Lippincott & Co., 1872.

———. *Naval Percussion Locks and Primers, Particularly those of the United States States*. Philadelphia: A. Hart, 1853.

———. "A Report of the Superintendent of Ordnance of the Washington Navy Yard on Rifled Cannon and the Armament of Ships of War." 36th Congress, 2d Session, Executive Document 25.

———. *Report on the Thirty-two Pounder or Thirty-two cwt. To Commodore Warrington, Chief of the Bureau of Ordnance and Hydrography, by Lieut. Jno. A. Dahlgren*. Washington, DC: C. Alexander, 1850.

———. "Rifled Cannon and the Armament of Ships-of-War." 36th Congress, 2d Session, House of Representatives, Ex. Doc. No. 43.

———. *Shells and Shell Guns*. Philadelphia: King and Baird, 1856.

———. *A System of Boat Armament in the United States Navy: Reported to Commodore Charles Morris*. Philadelphia: A. Hart, 1852.

Dahlgren, Madeleine Vinton. *Memoir of John A. Dahlgren: Rear-Admiral United States Navy*. Boston: James R. Osgood and Company, 1882.

Davis, W. W. H. *History of the 104th Pennsylvania Infantry Regiment, from August 22nd, 1861 to September 20th, 1864*. Philadelphia: James B. Rodgers, 1866.

De Kay, James Tertius. *Chronicles of the Frigate Macedonian: 1809-1922*. New York: W.W. Norton and Company, 1995.

Douglas, Sir Howard. *A Treatise on Naval Gunnery*. 5th Ed. London: John Murray, 1860.

Dudley, William S. *Going South: U.S. Navy Officer Resignations & Dismissals on the Eve of the Civil War*. Washington, DC: Naval Historical Foundation, 1981.

Dudley, William S., ed. *The Naval War of 1812: A Documentary History*, Volume 1. Washington, DC: Naval Historical Center, 1985.

Du Pont, Samuel Francis. *Samuel Francis Du Pont: A Selection from His Civil War*

Letters. Vol. 3, The Repulse: 1863-1865. Edited by John D. Hayes. Ithaca, NY: Published for the Eleutherian Mills Historical Library by Cornell University Press, 1969.

Fabian, Ann. *The Unvarnished Truth: Personal Narratives in Nineteenth-Century America*. Berkeley: University of California Press, 2000.

[Falconer, William.] *A New Universal Dictionary of the Marine...*, ed. William Burney. London: Joyce Gold, 1815.

Fonvielle, Chris E., Jr. *The Wilmington Campaign: Last Rays of Departing Hope.* Campbell, CA: Savas Publishing Company, 1997.

[Francis, Theodore Augustus.] *History of the 71st Regiment, N.G., N.Y.* New York: The Veterans Association, 71st Regiment, N.G.N.Y., 1919.

Fremantle, [Arthur James Lyon]. *Three Months in the Southern States: April–June, 1863.* New York: John Bradburn, 1864.

Fuller, Howard J. *Clad in Iron: The American Civil War and the Challenge of British Naval Power.* Westport, CT: Praeger, 2008.

Gienapp, William E. and Erica L. Gienapp, eds. *The Civil War Diary of Gideon Welles, Lincoln's Secretary of the Navy: The Original Manuscript Edition*. Urbana: The Knox College Lincoln Studies Center and the University of Illinois Press, 2014.

Gillmore, Q[uincy] A. *Engineer and Artillery Operations Against the Defences of Charleston Harbor in 1863; Comprising the Descent Upon Morris Island, the Demolition of Fort Sumter, the Reduction of Forts Wagner and Gregg. With Observations on Heavy Ordnance, Fortifications, Etc.* New York: D. Van Nostrand, 1865.

Grivel, Louis Antoine Richild. *Attaques et bombardements maritime avant et pendant la guerre d'Orient. Sébastopol.—Bomarsund.—Odessa—Sweaborg.—Kinburn*. 2nd. ed. Paris: J. Dumaine, 1857.

Hassler, F[erdinand] R[udolf]. *Principal Documents Relating to the Survey of the Coast of the United States, Since 1816*. New York: William van Norden, 1834.

Headley, J[oel] T[aylor]. *Farragut and Our Naval Commanders*. New York: E. B. Treat & Co., 1867.

Hoptak, John David. "The Union's First Defenders," *Pennsylvania Heritage* Vol. 39 No. 3 (Summer 2013): 5–15.

Joinville, Prince de. *Memoirs (Vieux Souvenirs) of the Prince de Joinville*, translated by Lady Mary Loyd. London: William Heinemann, 1895.

Kahan, Paul. *Amiable Scoundrel: Simon Cameron, Lincoln's Scandalous Secretary of War.* Lincoln, NE: Potomac Books, 2016.

Keehn, David C. *Knights of the Golden Circle: Secret Empire, Southern Secession, Civil*

War. Baton Rouge: Louisiana State University Press, 2013.

"Letter from the Secretary of War in Reference to Fortifications," 11 December 1851. 32d Congress, 1st Session, House Executive Document No. 5.

Long, David F. *Sailor Diplomat: A Biography of Commodore James Biddle, 1783-1848*. Boston: Northeastern University Press, 1983.

[Marshall, Jessie Ames, ed.] *Private and Official Correspondence of Gen. Benjamin F. Butler During the Period of the Civil War*, Vol. 3. Norwood, MA: Plimpton Press, 1917.

Miers, Earl Schenk and C. Percy Powell. *Lincoln Day by Day: A Chronology 1809–1865*. Dayton, OH: Morningside, 1991.

Morgan, William James, David B. Tyler, Joye L. Leonhart, and Mary F. Loughlin, eds. *Autobiography of Rear Admiral Charles Wilkes, U.S. Navy 1797–1877*. Washington, DC: Naval History Division, 1978.

Nicolay, John G. and John Hay. *Complete Works of Abraham Lincoln*, New and Enlarged Edition. Volume 7. N.p.: Lincoln Memorial University, 1894.

Official Records of the Union and Confederate Navies in the War of the Rebellion. 31 vols. Washington, DC: Government Printing Office, 1894–1922.

Parker, Foxhall. *The Naval Howitzer Ashore*. New York: D. Van Nostrand, 1865.

Paullin, Charles Oscar. *Paullin's History of Naval Administration 1775–1911: A Collection of Articles from the U.S. Naval Institute* Proceedings. Annapolis, MD: U.S. Naval Institute, 1968.

Peck, Taylor. *Round-Shot to Rockets: A History of the Washington Navy Yard and U.S. Naval Gun Factory*. Annapolis, MD: United States Naval Institute, 1949.

"Permanent Fortifications and Sea-Coast Defences." 23 April 1862. 37th Congress, 2d Session, House Report No. 86.

Pohanka, Brian C., and Patrick A. Schroeder, eds. *With the 11th New York Fire Zouaves In Camp, Battle, and Prison: The Narrative of Private Arthur O'Neil Alcock in* The New York Atlas and Leader. Lynchburg, VA: Schroeder Publications, 2011.

Potter, David M. *The Impending Crisis 1848–1861*. New York: Harper and Row, 1976.

Report of the Joint Committee on the Conduct of the War. 8 vols. Washington, DC: Government Printing Office, 1863–1866. Reprint; 9 vols., Wilmington, NC. Broadfoot Publishing Company, 2002.

Report of the Secretary of the Navy. [Washington, DC: Government Printing Office,] 1858.

Report of the Secretary of the Navy in Relation to Armored Vessels. Washington, DC: Government Printing Office, 1864.

Report of the Secretary of the Navy, with an Appendix Containing Reports from Officers. [Washington, DC: Government Printing Office,] 1865.

Scharf, J. Thomas. *History of the Confederate States Navy from Its Organization to the Surrender of Its Last Vessel.* 2nd ed. Albany, NY: Joseph McDonough, 1894.

Schneller, Robert J., Jr. *A Quest for Glory: A Biography of Rear Admiral John A. Dahlgren.* Annapolis, MD: Naval Institute Press, 1996.

Scott, Winfield. *Memoirs of Lieut.-General Winfield Scott*, ed. Timothy D. Johnson. 1864. Reprint, Knoxville: University of Tennessee Press, 2015.

Silverstone, Paul H. *Civil War Navies 1855–1883.* Annapolis, MD: Naval Institute Press, 2001.

Slotten, Hugh Richard. *Patronage, Practice, and the Culture of American Science: Alexander Dallas Bache and the U.S. Coast Survey.* New York: Cambridge University Press, 1994.

Smith, Gene A. *Thomas ap Catesby Jones: Commodore of Manifest Destiny.* Annapolis, MD: Naval Institute Press, 2000.

Spencer C. Tucker. *Andrew Foote: Civil War Admiral on Western Waters.* Annapolis, MD: Naval Institute Press, 2000.

———. *Arming the Fleet: U.S. Navy Ordnance in the Muzzle-Loading Era.* Annapolis, MD: Naval Institute Press, 1989.

Venter, Bruce M. *Kill Jeff Davis: The Union Raid on Richmond, 1864.* Norman: University of Oklahoma Press, 2016.

Warner, Ezra J. *Generals in Blue: Lives of the Union Commanders.* Baton Rouge: Louisiana State University Press, 1964.

———. *Generals in Gray: Lives of the Confederate Commanders.* Baton Rouge: Louisiana State University Press, 1959.

The War of the Rebellion: A Compilation of the Official Records of the Union and Confederate Armies. 128 vols. Washington, DC: Government Printing Office, 1880–1901.

Weddle, Kevin J. *Lincoln's Tragic Admiral: The Life of Samuel Francis Du Pont.* Charlottesville: University of Virginia Press, 2005.

Westwood, Howard C. "Ben Butler Takes on a Chaplain," *Civil War History* Vol. 35, No 3. (1989): 225–38.

INDEX

Letters in bold are photographs—**28**
"n" following number is footnote—28n9

About the Editor

Peter C. Luebke earned his PhD from the University of Virginia, where he studied United States military history. Before joining Naval History and Heritage Command (NHHC), he worked in historic preservation at the Virginia Department of Historic Resources and authored or coauthored several National Register of Historic Places nominations, including that of USS *Wisconsin* (BB-64). He was an associate editor for *A Grave Misfortune: The USS Indianapolis Tragedy*, a recent NHHC publication. Currently, he is an editor for the *Naval Documents of the American Revolution* project at NHHC.